# THIS IS
# MEXICO

Text by James Bowyer

Photographs by Mireille Vautier

NEW
HOLLAND

First published in 1999 by
New Holland Publishers (UK) Ltd
London • Cape Town • Sydney • Auckland

24 Nutford Place
London W1H 6DQ, United Kingdom

80 McKenzie Street
Cape Town 8001, South Africa

14 Aquatic Drive
Frenchs Forest, NSW 2086, Australia

218 Lake Road
Northcote, Auckland, New Zealand

ISBN 1 85974 095 2

Editor: Simon Pooley
Designer: Daniël Jansen van Vuuren
Consultant: Gabriela Canseco
Publishing Manager: Mariëlle Renssen
Cartography: Anton Krugel
Indexer: Annelene van der Merwe
Picture Researcher: Carmen Watts

Reproduction by Disc Express Cape (Pty) Ltd
Printed and bound in Singapore by
Tien Wah Press (Pte) Ltd

10 9 8 7 6 5 4 3 2 1

Illustrations appearing in the preliminary pages are
as follows:
HALF TITLE: Indian women buying pottery, Puebla.
FRONTISPIECE: The church of Nuestra Señora de
los Remedios, at Cholula.
TITLE PAGE: Boy wearing Aztec jaguar costume.
PAGE 4: Salt mines on the Baja California Peninsula,
and Indian weaving from Chiapas.
PAGES 6 and 7: Red, Green and Scarlet Macaws.

## ACKNOWLEDGEMENTS

The author wishes to thank a number of organiza-
tions who helped in creating this book. First and
foremost is the Mexican Embassy in South Africa,
and in particular David Ibarra, who offered invaluable advice and support. South African Airways,
Aeromexico, Aerocaribe and Mexicana Airways all
provided valuable assistance. I would also like to
thank Derek Schuurman for all his help, and Lu
Dowell for her advice and support.

The Editor would like to thank Cara Cilliers for
additional photographic research, Tim Jollands for
editorial input, and Tony Pooley for contacts and
information on Mexican fauna.

# Contents

# THIS IS
# MEXICO

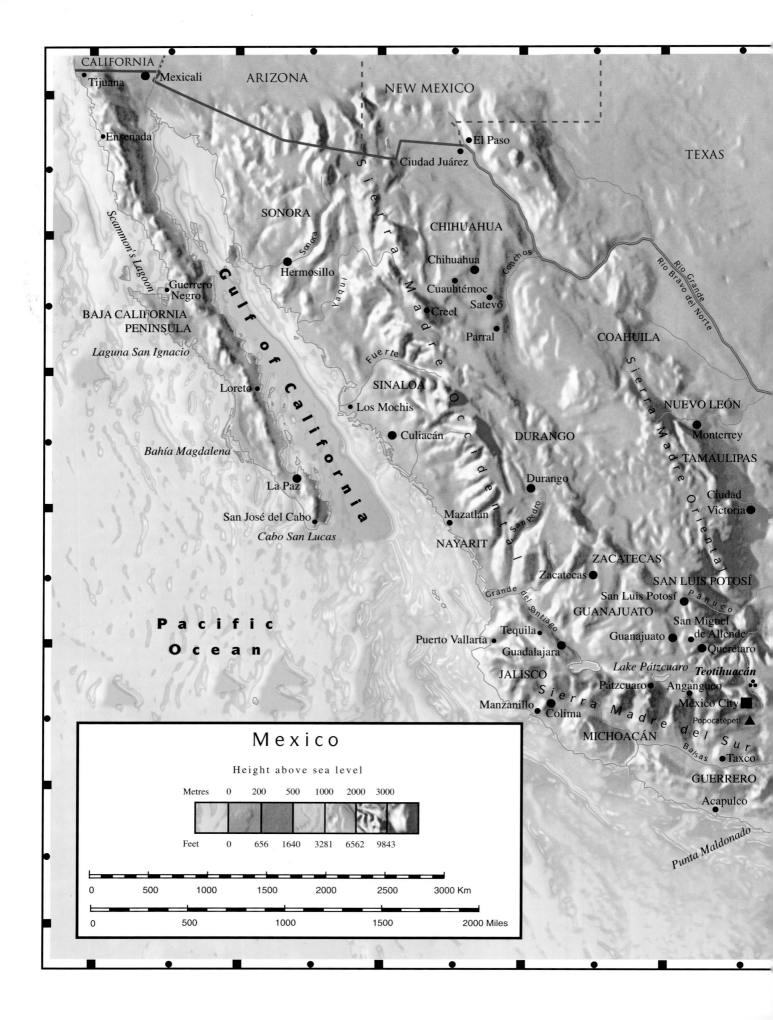

CALIFORNIA
Tijuana
Mexicali
ARIZONA
NEW MEXICO
Ensenada
El Paso
Ciudad Juárez
TEXAS

SONORA
CHIHUAHUA
Chihuahua
Cuauhtémoc
Satevó
Hermosillo
Creel
Parral
COAHUILA

BAJA CALIFORNIA
PENINSULA
Laguna San Ignacio
Scammon's Lagoon
Guerrero
Negro

Sierra Madre Occidental
Sonora
Yaqui
Fuerte
Conchos

Rio Grande
Rio Bravo del Norte

Gulf of California

SINALOA
Loreto
Los Mochis
DURANGO
NUEVO LEÓN
Culiacán
Monterrey
TAMAULIPAS

Bahía Magdalena
Durango
Ciudad
Victoria

La Paz
San José del Cabo
Mazatlán
San Pedro
Cabo San Lucas
NAYARIT

Sierra Madre Oriental
Pánuco

ZACATECAS
Zacatecas
SAN LUIS POTOSÍ
San Luis Potosí
GUANAJUATO
San Miguel
de Allende
Guanajuato
Querétaro

Grande del Santiago
Pacific
Ocean
Tequila
Puerto Vallarta
Guadalajara
Lake Pátzcuaro
Teotihuacán
JALISCO
Pátzcuaro
Angangueo
Sierra Madre del Sur
Manzanillo
Colima
Mexico City
Popocatépetl ▲
MICHOACÁN
Balsas
Taxco

GUERRERO
Acapulco

Punta Maldonado

# Mexico

Height above sea level

| Metres | 0 | 200 | 500 | 1000 | 2000 | 3000 |
|---|---|---|---|---|---|---|

| Feet | 0 | 656 | 1640 | 3281 | 6562 | 9843 |
|---|---|---|---|---|---|---|

| 0 | 500 | 1000 | 1500 | 2000 | 2500 | 3000 Km |
|---|---|---|---|---|---|---|

| 0 | 500 | 1000 | 1500 | 2000 Miles |
|---|---|---|---|---|

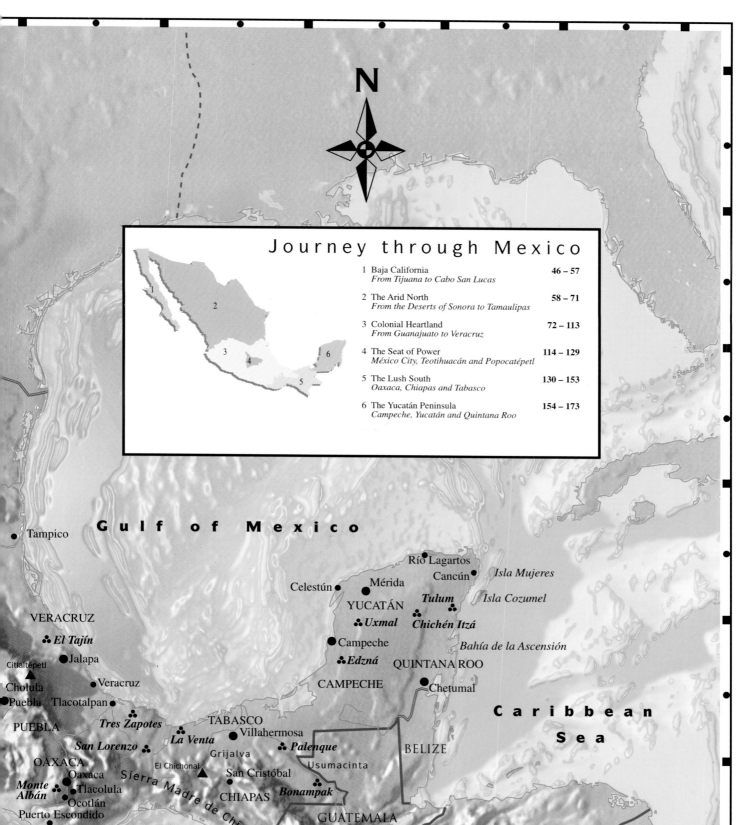

# Journey through Mexico

**N**

Tampico

**G u l f   o f   M e x i c o**

Río Lagartos
Cancún
Celestún    Mérida              Isla Mujeres
**YUCATÁN**                     Isla Cozumel
            **Tulum**
♣ **Uxmal**  **Chichén Itzá**

♣ **El Tajín**
Citlaltépetl    Jalapa        Campeche          Bahía de la Ascensión
**VERACRUZ**          ♣ **Edzná**   **QUINTANA ROO**
Cholula    Veracruz      **CAMPECHE**    Chetumal
Puebla   Tlacotalpan

**PUEBLA**   **Tres Zapotes**   **TABASCO**                     **C a r i b b e a n**
          **San Lorenzo**  ♣ **La Venta**   Villahermosa                   **S e a**
**OAXACA**              Grijalva    ♣ **Palenque**
Oaxaca     El Chichonal    San Cristóbal    **BELIZE**
**Monte**  Tlacolula      Usumacinta
**Albán**  Ocotlán   **CHIAPAS**   **Bonampak**
Puerto Escondido        Sierra Madre de Chiapas   **GUATEMALA**
Puerto Ángel   Huatulco                           **HONDURAS**
                Tacaná Volcano

**G u l f   o f**

**T e h u a n t e p e c**

# PROFILE OF MEXICO

Mexico is a country forever in flux. Its history is as turbulent as its landscape which tumbles and falls, often exploding into spectacular and devastating eruptions. Mexico has survived the shock of European invasion, 300 years of colonial rule, war with the USA, civil war and three cruel decades of dictatorship. The 'children of the shaking earth', as Mexico's people are known, have endured their trembling land and perennial wars with a stoicism unique to this nation.

The country's landscape is extreme. It is a land characterized by plunging gorges and soaring mountains, studded with towering volcanoes that continue to shape the land. Half of Mexico falls inside of the tropics, the other half within dry arid areas, resulting in extreme contrasts between the desert areas of the north and the rainforests of the south. The meeting of these factors within one country makes Mexico an incredibly complex territory, rich in vegetation, wildlife and breathtaking vistas.

This diverse country has seeded a great variety of cultures. The Olmec civilization, the first of the great Mesoamerican cultures, emerged about 3500 years ago. They were succeeded by the Maya, the Toltecs and the Aztecs. The history and development of Mexico's ancient cultures was abruptly cut short by the arrival of the Spanish Conquistadors in 1519. This traumatic meeting between Mesoamerican and early 16th-century European cultures resulted in the painful birth of the Mexican nation.

Popocatépetl, a brooding volcano, stands sentinel over the largest city in the world as nearly one-sixth of Mexico's populace prepare to face another day. Although the 5465m (17,930ft) snow-capped volcano has not had a major eruption since 1802, it is by no means dormant. Occasional gasps of steam are dire reminders of the subterranean forces at work shaping this dynamic land.

The people of México City appear to be oblivious to the dangers of living beneath an active volcano and the city continues to spin at its own frantic pace. More than 20 million people live within the greater metropolitan area of Mexico DF, the *Distrito Federal*, or México as it is known by its people. The world's largest metropolitan area is also one of the world's fastest growing, and staggering population predictions of up to 30 million people are forecast for the year 2000.

At the epicentre of this frenzy you will find the central plaza or square which is the heartbeat of any Mexican town or city. Here Mariachi bands weave their way through sidewalk cafés exchanging songs for a few pesos while shoe-shiners and colourful balloon-sellers turn a brisk trade. This is Mexico, a land of contrasts, where colours seem to be brighter than usual. It is a feast for the senses, often chilli-hot, never bland.

# THE LAND

Mexico resembles a vast horn, curving away from North America and tapering off into South America. Physically, it is a bridge between North and South America, linking the continents and separating the Pacific from the Atlantic Ocean. During early geological times, the ocean separated these two continents and much of Mexico, as we know it today, was submerged. The Isthmus of Tehuantepec that now joins North and South America was formed during the Pliocene age, two to five million years ago.

Mexico is the largest of the Central American countries, covering an area of 1,953,162km$^2$ (753,920 sq. miles), of which 6006km$^2$ (2318 sq. miles) is made up of islands. The north of the country shares a 3117km-long (1937-mile) border with the USA, which at its most northerly point reaches a northern latitude of 32° 43 27. The south of the country shares a 1192km-long (740-mile) border with Guatemala and Belize and reaches its southernmost point at the mouth of the Suchiate River at a northern latitude of 14° 32 27.

Mexico's eastern extent lies off the Yucatán Peninsula, on the southeastern edge of the small 8km-long (5-mile) Mujeres Island in the Caribbean Sea, at a western longitude of 86° 42 36. The most westerly co-ordinate falls on Guadeloupe, an island in the Pacific Ocean, at a longitude of 118° 27 24 west. Mexico's coastline, not including that of its islands, stretches for an impressive 11,590km (7200 miles).

## The Baja California Peninsula

One of the country's most interesting geological features is the Baja California Peninsula, a rocky 1290km-long (800-mile) finger of arid land that appears to have fallen off from the rest of the country. With less than 250mm (10in) of rain a year, the Peninsula has long refused to be inhabited and today remains sparsely populated. It is largely a land of mountains interspersed with deserts that are framed with pristine beaches. In the north, near the border with the USA, is the Laguna de los Volcanes, or Volcano Lake, an active volcanic field that spews out boiling mud and provides clues to the peninsula's geological past. The explosions of the volcanic field are reminders of the violent subterranean forces that created the entire Peninsula

*The Baja California Peninsula* (above).
*Nopal (Prickly Pear) Cactus country* (left).

PREVIOUS PAGES:
PAGE 10: *Mexico's* Voladores *or 'Flying Men' performing at the festival of Corpus Christi, in Papantla.*
PAGE 11: *A couple of Tlacoleros celebrate their festival in vibrant costumes.*

*Pine forests form a striking contrast to Mexico's arid regions. With 22 species and varieties of pine occurring at higher altitudes, Mexico has more pine species than any other country.*

and surrounding islands. Beneath the Peninsula's rugged surface is the continuation of the great fracture in the earth's crust known as the San Andreas Fault. More than 20 million years ago extreme pressure along this fault caused the Peninsula to break off from the Mexican mainland. Since then the Peninsula has crept in a northwesterly direction and has moved about 400km (250 miles) away from the mainland. The powerful forces that moulded the Peninsula continue to send tremors across the land.

## The Mainland

Mexico's dominant characteristic is its mountains. There is a story about the country's geography that is revealing. When asked by King Carlos V to describe New Spain, the Spanish king's prized new territory, Conquistador Hernán Cortés crumpled up a piece of paper and handed it to the king. Mexico is a crumpled land where to travel is to cross mountains. With the exception of the northern deserts and the Yucatán Peninsula, there are few areas out of sight of some peak or other.

Mexico's mountains are made up of four major ranges, namely the Sierra Madre Occidental, the Sierra Madre Oriental, the Sierra Madre del Sur and the Sierra Madre de Chiapas. Over 60 per cent of the country is located within the 'Mesa Central', or Central Plateau, a rugged highland area bordered by the 1290km-long (800-mile) Sierra Madre Occidental in the west and the lesser Sierra Madre Oriental in the east.

The two Sierras are the backbone of the country. Together they build the Central Plateau that rises an average of 1200m (3937ft) above sea level in the north to 2400m (7874ft) in the south. Many of the rivers in this area drain into interior basins, chiselling out deep, dramatic canyons (*barrancas*), that easily rival those of the better known Grand Canyon in the USA in both size and beauty. This northern landscape is dominated by vast deserts lined with spiny mountains.

Central Mexico is crowned by a ring of towering, widely spaced volcanoes known as the Sierra Volcanica Transversal which has long dominated the land and people of this area. This is roughly where the country's two northern mountain ranges meet, marking a band of intense seismic activity.

Further south the land turns lumpy as the Central Plateau rises to meet the Sierra Madre del Sur which runs along the Pacific coast in a southeasterly direction through Guerrero State and into Oaxaca. The mountains continue to tumble on southwards, subside temporarily around the swampy Isthmus of Tehuantepec, then roll on into the rainforests of southern Mexico. Here the Sierra Madre de Chiapas crosses from the state of Chiapas south into Guatemala.

## The Yucatán Peninsula

To the east of the country is the Yucatán Peninsula, a low-lying area predominantly made up of layers of limestone rock resting on a crystalline base. Here underground streams and lakes burrow deep beneath the surface limestone, providing water for the people of the area. Relatively speaking, this region is a geological youngster, having only recently emerged from beneath the waves of the Gulf of Mexico.

Thus, Mexico's varied territory includes an isthmus, a continental mass, a number of islands and two peninsulas.

*The glaciated slopes of Pico de Orizaba, also known as Citlaltépetl (Mountain of the Stars in Náhuatl), which is Mexico's highest mountain. It dominates Mexico's volcanic 'Ring of Fire'.*

## Seismic Activity

Adding complexity to the patterns of this changing land are the unseen forces of grinding tectonic plates and the very visible effects of spectacular volcanoes and devastating earthquakes. Mexico is located within one of the world's more unstable geographic zones and is often witness to intense earth movement. The people of Mexico are accustomed to the hazards of life on shaky ground. As recently as 1985, México City was brought to a standstill by a devastating earthquake that claimed an estimated 10,000 lives and caused immeasurable damage. Throughout the long history of human settlement in Mexico's central volcanic belt, there is hardly a town or city that has not felt the wrath of an earthquake or volcanic eruption.

The seismic activity is evidence of the Pacific Ocean's Coco plate moving beneath the North American and Caribbean plates, part of the aptly named Pacific 'Ring of Fire'. The highest of these volcanoes is Pico de Orizaba, also know as Citlaltépetl, which at 5747m (18,855ft), is also the highest peak in Central America. Also part of this chain is Popocatépetl, the brooding 5465m

(17,930ft) snow-capped peak that overlooks México City.

Mexico's most recent eruption of note was the angry work of El Chichónal, in the southern state of Chiapas. The volcano's 1982 eruption sent a 17km-long

(10-mile) plume of ash and smoke into the air. The cloud drifted westwards and in less than a year had circled the globe. So great was the cloud that it is believed to have caused freak weather conditions in the Pacific region and a cooling of up to 2°C (35.6°F) in some areas. Paradoxically, this unstable zone is rich in fertile volcanic soils that have, for centuries, supported the cultivation of crops and livestock in the highland areas of Mexico. It was an abundance of fertile soil that first encouraged people to inhabit the Central Valley, and so the seed that would become the Mesoamerican cultures was planted.

## Islands

Most of Mexico's islands exist as little-known worlds, yet to be explored or exploited. Recently some of them have been conscripted into Mexico's growing tourism industry. Californian Sea Lions and goats are the only inhabitants of the islands off the Baja California Peninsula, while islands off Cancún and Cozumel, on the Yucatán Peninsula, are important tourist developments.

*Mexico includes over 6000 km² (2300 sq. miles) of island territory. Much of this, like the island above in the Gulf of California, is inhabited only by goats and sea lions.*

# CLIMATE

Mexico, claim its tourist brochures, has a 'privileged climate'. It is a claim that is difficult to dispute. Overall, Mexico's climate is benign; it does not move too radically between the extremes. However, in character with the nature of the country, Mexico's climate has a way of surprising.

Officially, summer runs from June to October. In theory this is the rainy season, but regional differences in climate exert great influence over the seasons. The central areas of the country face short, heavy afternoon rainfalls virtually every day in the rainy season, while in the north hardly any rain falls at all. In the south and in many of the low-lying coastal areas, summers are humid and sticky. The sweltering heat is broken only by the occasional spectacular thunderstorm.

The latitude at which Mexico is located, its extensive coastlines and the varied topography make possible an extraordinary variety of macro- and microclimates. These range from Mediterranean to humid tropical climates; from the hottest deserts to frigid tundra; and include just about every other kind of temperate climate in between.

Microclimates are common throughout the country and are encountered with unexpected regularity. Given the country's mountain-dominated terrain, drastic changes in elevation and climate are common over short distances. It is possible to drive great distances along the Pacific coastline and experience little variation in the weather, but turn inland into the mountain areas and conditions change quickly.

Mexico's greatest climatic influences are latitude and altitude. The diversity of these influences adds complexity to what is essentially a temperate climate. As a rough rule of thumb, in areas with an altitude of less than 1000m (3281ft) above sea level, the climate is determined by latitude. Mexico is bisected latitudinally by the Tropic of Cancer,

*The Valle de los Angeles, in the Baja California Peninsula, falls within the* tierra caliente, *Mexico's hot lands, where temperatures often rise to around 30℃ (86°F).*

which divides the country at a point north of Cabo San Lucas, on the tip of the Baja California Peninsula. The land north of the line of the Tropics is dry, characterized by deserts where only cacti can thrive. The coastal plains skirting the country and the foothills of the sierras are the *tierra caliente*, the 'hot lands'. Much of this area falls below 1000m (3281ft) and temperatures here

*A climber steps across a land of ice on the upper slopes of Popocatépetl Volcano and enters the* tierra helada, *Mexico's frozen lands ruled by snow-capped peaks.*

*Bougainvillaea* (top) *and Poinsettia flowers* (above) *are common in Mexico.*

are usually a sweltering 30°C (86°F). Between August and October it is not uncommon to experience tropical hurricanes in these areas.

In higher zones, those above 1000m (3281ft), the climate is determined by altitude with the temperature gradient decreasing with height and reduced rainfall. This is the *tierra templada*, the 'temperate land', which makes up the central and northern areas of the country (about 28 per cent of the territory). Here rainfall ranges between 300 and 600mm (11 and 23in) a year and average temperatures hover around 18 to 26°C (64 to 78°F). In the far north, low rainfall and extremes in the daily temperature gradient produce a desert-like landscape. Above 2000m (6562ft) is the *tierra fria*, the 'cold lands' and above this are the *tierra helada*, the 'frozen lands', where the mercury seldom creeps above 10°C (50°F).

South of the Tropics is the country's high rainfall area. About 1.5 billion m³

(52 billion ft³) of rain falls over Mexico each year. If spread equally across the country, 75cm (30in) of water would cover the entire surface area of the country. This is not the case and intense rainfall is limited to specific areas, the southern states getting the brunt of it. In some areas yearly rainfall is measured not in centimetres but in metres, and it is not uncommon for minor roads to be washed away by excessive downpours. Rainfall increases in a southeasterly direction with the heaviest rain falling along the coast of the Gulf of Mexico and southern regions.

Roughly 23 per cent of the country has a warm sub-humid climate with an annual rainfall of between 1000 and 2000mm (39 and 78in) and a temperature range of between 22 and 26°C (71 and 78°F). This is the tropical belt that skirts much of southern Mexico's coastline, including the Yucatán Peninsula.

Winters are generally dry. This is usually the tourist season, but Mexico's climate and people welcome visitors all year round. Tourists generally stick to the cooler highlands in summer and the warm coastal lowlands in winter.

# FLORA AND FAUNA

Few countries can claim to have such an abundance of life forms as does Mexico. The territory is one of the world's most bio-diverse, boasting the 4th- or 5th-highest species count of any country in the world. Ten per cent of the world's known species occur within this relatively small territory, which comprises about 1.5 per cent of the world's total land surface area.

Mexico has the world's greatest number of reptile species for any one country, and is second only to Indonesia in numbers of land mammal species. It has the fourth-largest concentration of higher plant species (around 20,000) on earth. Examples of practically all of the world's ecosystems can be found within its borders. The reasons for this abundance of life are many, one of the most

*The highlands of northern Mexico are covered in pine forests, such as these hills near Toluca Volcano (in the background).*

important being the country's geographical location. As a bridge between the Americas the country is situated between two very different climatic regions, namely the boreal (snowy winters and short summers) region of North America and the tropical region of South America. As a mid-point between climatic zones, Mexico became a refuge for many species escaping extreme climatic shifts. During the glacial period of the Pleistocene era, the most recent of the earth's great climatic upheavals, species migrated from the North and South Americas to escape the intense cold. Many settled in the relatively mild territory today known as Mexico. With the end of the Ice Age the reverse happened, with many species migrating north or southwards, once again crossing into and settling in Mexico. Over

tens of thousands of years the exotic creatures adapted themselves to the habitats of the region.

The country's endemic species form an unusually large part of the region's fauna and flora; about half of the country's species of reptiles and amphibians are unique to Mexico. The same holds for a third of the country's mammals.

The considerable bio-diversity within the country is partly a result of its turbulent geological history. Unusual physical landscapes, combined with a broad latitudinal sweep and long coastlines, have given rise to a profusion of microclimates ranging from bleak tundra-like deserts to humid tropical zones. Between these extremes a range of climates provide suitable environments for a wide diversity of life forms.

While the value of such biological wealth may seem obvious, the destruction of Mexico's environment is one of the biggest issues facing the country. The effects of rapid population growth, industrial activity and development are

taking their toll. Sadly, what is being destroyed and lost has yet to be fully documented or understood. Biologists claim that our knowledge of the world's species amounts to less than 10 per cent of what is estimated to be the true count. Mexico is no different in this regard. The country's biological wealth has yet to be fully explored, let alone documented. An example of this is the 'discovery' of a new plant species, the *Lacandonia schismatica*, in the Chiapas jungle – the first discovery of a new family of higher plants since 1942. The most recent family of plants to be discovered was the Ticodendraceae. This family was identified in 1991, and its range extends from Oaxaca State to Panama.

## FLORA

Mexico is home to 32 major vegetation types, comprising more than 20,000 species of flora. Such diversity in a single country is rare and only occurs in ecologically privileged areas such as India, Peru and Australia. Great ranges in rainfall, temperature, topography and a wide variety of fauna and soil types have all contributed to this floristic diversity.

There is, broadly speaking, an identifiable pattern in Mexico's floristic distribution. The greater density of species occurs in the warm, humid areas, south of the Tropic of Cancer. Most of these species are found in the tropical forests, such as Los Tuxtlas in Veracruz or the Lacandón rainforests in the south. The count of floral species occurring in the jungles of Los Tuxtlas alone is only slightly less than that for the entire British Isles.

### Forests

Many centuries ago, much of Mexico was covered by vast forests, but deforestation has dramatically escalated in the past few centuries. This is particularly due to the proliferation of cattle ranches and the extraction of precious woods. Logging companies, armed with indiscriminate concessions to work the forests, have destroyed huge areas of the indigenous woodlands. Nevertheless,

*The wild northern Sierra mountains are the last refuge for the Mexican Wolf (top), which faces extinction. Nine-banded Armadillos (above) occur in the Yucatán Peninsula. The local Indians eat them.*

Mexico's forest resources are still relatively large. Out of a total of 192 million ha (474 million acres) of land area, over a quarter consists of woodlands, an area that accounts for about 1.3 per cent of the world's total forested area.

The temperate-cold climates in the central and northern highland areas of Mexico are dominated by coniferous (mostly pine) and broad-leaved species, which account for about 26 million ha (64 million acres) of the country's woodland area. Pines are well suited to Mexico as much of the country is situated over 1000m (3281ft). The country has 72 species, varieties and forms of pine, more than any other country in the world.

Tropical and subtropical forests, which are mainly situated in the southern areas, account for about 24 million ha (59 million acres) of woodlands. In contrast to the production from coniferous

*The Lacandón forests at the Montes Azules Reserve in Chiapas are some of Mexico's last remaining rainforests. They are a haven for rare species including orchids and jaguars.*

*Totonac farmers practise age-old farming techniques on their corn field in Veracruz.*

forests, the tropical forests make up only 10 per cent of Mexico's total forest production. Although Mexico's forest area is large, the production of wood contributes only 0.6 per cent to the country's gross domestic product. This is partly due to the inaccessibility of the forest areas and the poor infrastructure in these areas. As a result the cost of wood production in Mexico is 35 to 40 per cent higher than the world average.

**Forest Farmers**

Biologists claim that there is a direct link between the biological diversity of an area and the discovery of cultivated plants – in other words, the agriculture that many early societies depended on.

The biological wealth of the Mesoamerican region has provided the world with a variety of cultivated plants that today feed millions of people. Mexico's contribution to food types is disproportionately large. Examples include many varieties of corn, tomatoes, beans, squash, chillis, avocados, tomatoes, cacao and vanilla.

Many of these plants were first found in Mexico's woodland areas where there has been a long tradition of forestry dating back to the earliest Mesoamerican civilizations. The Maya, the first forest farmers, lived for centuries within the Lacandón jungle in the state of Chiapas, part of an area that is today known as the Gran Petén. After the Amazon, this is the second-largest rainforest zone in the Central and South American regions.

Today, descendants of these early forest farmers continue to harvest the Lacandón forests, practising age-old cultivation methods that rely on a deep knowledge of the sensitive forest ecology. The key to surviving in the forest areas is a farming technique known as slash-and-burn agriculture. Farmers begin by clearing, in spring, one-hectare (2.4-acre) plots. The vegetation is dried and then burnt in a controlled manner. There is good reason for this seemingly destructive practice. In the tropical forests, the majority of nutrients are generally suspended in the forest canopy, and only the uppermost layers

of the soil are rich in nutrients. Lacandón farmers release the nutrients contained in the trees by burning the vegetation, allowing the nutrient-rich ash to be absorbed into the soil.

Crops are planted during the six-month rainy season that follows the clearing of the land. Up to 80 varieties of food and fibre crops are then planted in a random manner that mimics the diversity of the surrounding forests. The randomness of the forest vegetation inhibits the spread of plant-specific diseases and prevents plagues of tropical insects. After the first crops are harvested, slower-growing crops such as papaya fruit trees are planted. In this way the land rejuvenates itself.

With careful weeding small, one hectare (2.4-acre) plots could provide sustenance for up to 25 years for a small Mayan family. After this period the family typically moved on and began clearing another plot of land. This subtle knowledge of the ways of the forests helped the Lacandón Maya survive in what is essentially a hostile environment.

*Spices, Mexico's essential ingredient. Mexico has contributed much to the world's palate.*

*White-tail Deer migrated south to Mexico.*

The small scale and controlled use of slash-and-burn farming proved to be sustainable. Unfortunately this technique has been corrupted by large-scale cattle farming. Millions of hectares of rainforest are cleared with slash-and-burn techniques to make way for cattle farming. In this way the cyclical nature of earlier farming techniques is broken and the land is soon sapped of nutrients.

It is estimated that some 25 per cent of Mexico's higher plant species are made use of, and according to the World Health Organisation, 85 per cent of the population still use herbal medicines. Much of this knowledge has its roots deeply embedded in thousands of years of Mesoamerican culture. Today, the keepers of much of this knowledge are the country's native Indians. It is estimated that Indians living in the tropical rainforests today use up to 1500 plant species to produce over 3000 different products. But like Mexico's biological wealth this knowledge is in danger of disappearing with the pressure of urbanization and the intrusion of economic imperatives into traditional lifestyles.

## Protecting Biodiversity

The need to protect the world's biological diversity is becoming ever more apparent, especially in a country as well-endowed as Mexico. Unfortunately, economic pressures have often eclipsed concerns about Mexico's dwindling bio-diversity.

Ecologists working in tropical areas maintain that the best way to preserve endangered areas is to find sustainable ways of exploiting them. In Mexico, policymakers appear to be looking to the past for successful solutions for today's problems. Until the 1930s foreign companies were given concessions to log Mexico's tropical forests, resulting in the massive destruction of sensitive jungle ecosystems. Eventually foreign companies were excluded, but logging by Mexican companies continued unchecked. However, in the 1980s local Indian communities were once again entrusted with the management of these jungle areas. A new Agrarian Law placed the forests in the hands of *ejidatarios*, collectives made up of forest farmers. These farmers were responsible to the government, but may now sell their land.

*Ejido* members use techniques similar to those of the early Maya. First, an inventory of the forest's resources is made. Then the forest area is divided into lots and wood is extracted from chosen lots on a rotational basis, allowing other areas to rejuvenate. These steps towards sustainable forest production have proven to be highly successful. They have won the Mexican government international forest management awards and may help preserve Mexico's valuable woodlands.

Another unusual ally in the struggle to preserve Mexico's forests are multinational pharmaceutical companies, which make use of natural organisms as raw products for medicines – or synthesize natural products for the formulation of new medicines. As our knowledge of Mexico's tropical forests accumulates, pharmaceutical companies have begun to take a keen interest in their future preservation. It is hoped that with sustained forest management and the emerging awareness of the forests' value, Mexico's – and the world's – precious resource will survive.

## FAUNA

Mexico has a disproportionately high collection of animal species. There are 717 different species of reptiles in Mexico, the highest tally recorded for any country in the world. Australia, ranked second in the world, has 597 species of reptiles. In terms of mammals, Mexico is host to 440 species, second only to Indonesia. Mexico can count 1150 bird species, out of the world's 9198 registered bird species.

For the past five million years, Mexico has formed a bridge between the two Americas, an evolutionary causeway along which the creatures of two continents crossed and settled. As a link between North and South America, Mexico is the meeting place of two very distinct faunistic regions that loosely

*An iguana – these reptiles have become rare in parts as some Mexicans eat them.*

converge along the Tropic of Cancer. To the north is the Neartic region typical to most of North America. The main ecosystems found in this region are desert scrublands, grasslands and temperate forests. Here, among other species, large bovids such as bison, and members of the deer family occur.

The Neotropical region, that of South America, extends into parts of southern Mexico and is characterized by warm, tropical areas. Typical creatures found in this region are marsupials, like the opossum. Also occurring here are the camelidae such as the llama, and the perissodactyls, such as the tapir.

A number of migratory species are drawn to Mexican wintering sites during the North American winter months. One of the most colourful of these is the Monarch Butterfly which migrates from parts of the USA to forests in the state of Michoacán. Some of the butterflies travel more than 3200km (2000 miles) during their incredible migration.

### Reptiles

It is not surprising that amongst Mexico's high count of reptile species there are a number of unique and interesting creatures. One of the rarest of these is Morelet's Crocodile. Mexico is also home to the American Crocodile, about 19 species of venomous coral snakes, two poisonous lizards, many species of rattlesnakes and dozens of turtle species.

In the Baja California Peninsula alone there are 18 species of rattlesnakes. The most common of these is the Lower California Rattlesnake, which is found throughout the Peninsula. Another of the Baja California Peninsula's common snakes is the Red Diamond. One of the region's more remarkable snakes is a rattlesnake that has no rattle. The snake, *Crotalus catalinensis,* was first found by biologists in 1952. At first the specimen was thought to be a rare deformity, but later specimens have confirmed the existence of this peculiar 'rattleless' rattlesnake.

*Blue-striped Grunt in the Gulf of California.*

### Marine Life

Mexico's abundant coastline is rich in marine life. In particular, the remoteness of Baja California, coupled with nutrient-rich seas has provided ideal conditions for underwater life. These waters are particularly favoured by whales.

There are 586 known species of fish in the Gulf of California alone. This strip of ocean separating the peninsula from the mainland is dominated by great currents caused by the flow and ebb of tides that push and pull water into and out of the Gulf. This perpetual motion ensures that these waters have a high oxygen level, ideal for microscopic animals or plants such as plankton which form a crucial first link in the marine food chain. Fish found here include marlin, big sea bass, giant groupers, yellowtails and the beautiful multicoloured dorado.

On the Pacific side of the peninsula the waters are less protected but are still rich in marine life. Here the region's remoteness has allowed species to thrive untouched by growing environmental pressures experienced in other parts of Mexico. The Guadeloupe Fur Seal, the Gray Whale and the Elephant Seal have all managed to fight off looming extinction and have successfully re-established themselves in this area.

In recent years the Baja Peninsula has become the focus of Mexico's thriving sport-fishing industry. A number of resorts here and along the Pacific coastline, like Manzanillo, offer facilities for hunting big-game species such as marlin, roosterfish and Yellowfin Tuna. La Paz, in Baja California, is the centre of Mexico's sportfishing effort, offering marinas, charter boat hire and modern hotels.

The Yucatán Peninsula, facing the Caribbean, has also become fashionable for fishing enthusiasts. The resort of Cancún is the hub of the industry here.

Mexico's largest fishing fleets harvest the warm waters of the Gulf of Mexico. At Veracruz almost 12,000 boats leave before dawn each day in search of shrimp, clams, oysters, crabs and fish.

### The Gray Whale

One of Mexico's natural wonders is the Gray Whale, *Rachinestes glaucus*. These graceful Leviathans have chosen the tranquil waters off the Baja Peninsula as their nursery grounds. During summer months the whales travel along the American Pacific seaboard to the Bering Sea where they feed on the abundant krill. When the days begin to shorten and the ice packs begin to form, the whales return to the Gulf of California and the breeding lagoons of the Baja Peninsula round trip is the longest recorded migratory route undertaken by a mammal.

Mexico has not always been so welcoming to the Gray Whale. Less than 150 years ago the breeding grounds of this species were discovered by whalers with devastating consequences. Until then, the grounds had been hidden within a vast lagoon, making them almost invisible from the sea. Their discovery by Charles Melville Scammon almost led to the extinction of the Gray Whale. Within years the whale population had been decimated.

In 1972, however, the whales' struggle for survival was greatly aided by the establishment of the world's first whale sanctuary at Scammon's Bay, ironically named after the whaler whose discovery caused so much damage. In that same year the hunting of the Gray Whale was banned with the implementation of the US Marine Mammals Protection act. In 1988 the whales were given more

*Whale-watchers reach out to touch a curious Gray Whale at Scammon's Lagoon on the west coast of the Baja California Peninsula. The waters of the Gulf of California are also famous for whales, and Blue, Sei, Humpback and Killer Whales can also be seen.*

protection when the sanctuary was expanded to include the Biosfera El Vizcaino National Park. This huge 2,546,790ha (6,293,120-acre) reserve now protects Gray Whales as well as a number of other unique species. Each year a quarter of a million tourists make their way to the Peninsula to observe the Gray Whales breeding. There are now around 20,000 Gray Whales.

*Blue Heron, Baja California Peninsula.*

*An Osprey hoists its hefty catch aloft.*

## Animals in Mesoamerican Mythology

Many of the Mesoamerican gods were associated with animals. A commonly held belief was that people could transform themselves into certain animals and in so doing assume the attributes of that animal.

The jaguar was widely worshipped and was an important Olmec god. The animal's image has been found carved into ceremonial axes and altars while jaguar masks and small jaguar figures, worked in fine jade, were buried with priests. The jaguar god did not disappear with the demise of the Olmecs. Other Mesoamerican groups, including the Toltecs, the Maya and the Aztecs paid homage to this swift-footed creature.

The Maya also honoured other creatures. One of these was the Quetzal, a colourful bird found in Mexico's southern tropical forests. The Maya trapped these beautiful birds and plucked out their emerald-green feathers to make headdresses and the great cloaks the Mayan leaders were buried in. The birds

*Jaguar and cattle masks worn by Indians show the importance of these animals in Indian belief systems, something that has persisted to this day.*

were then released to grow more feathers, and it was a capital offense to kill one. One of the most important of the Mesoamerican gods was Quetzalcóatl, the Plumed Serpent. This deity was a hybrid creature, a combination of the Quetzal and the rattlesnake. Now the Quetzal's numbers have dwindled drastically, and this bright bird has retreated into the thick jungles of Chiapas in Mexico, and other Central American countries.

The Olmecs and Maya were not alone in their worship of animals. The Aztecs' main god was Huitzilopochtli. The word *Huitzel* translates as 'hummingbird', and the story of the god's birth further links this fearful deity to the tiny bird. In Aztec mythology, a woman was impregnated by a ball of feathers she found while cleaning a temple. The feathers were presumably those of the hummingbird, and the offspring that this woman produced was a fully grown warrior, who appeared from her womb bearing a sword and the head of a serpent. He then proceeded to slay his sister and brothers, who had been planning to kill

him as he was the illegitimate offspring of their mother. They subsequently became the moon and the stars. Huitzilopochtli became the Aztecs' War God, Hunting God and Sun God.

# HISTORY

About 50,000 years ago, at a time when Alaska and Siberia were joined, the first inhabitants of the Americas migrated across the Bering Straits. Successive waves of these nomadic Stone Age hunters continued to filter into North America over the next 40,000 years. The new arrivals exerted pressure on settled groups, pushing settlements southwards, forcing communities to eventually filter into Central America.

In Mexico, the earliest evidence of human life has been found in the central areas of the country, known as the Central Valley. The first humans crossed this area about 20,000 years ago. In the 1940s the skeleton of one of the region's early inhabitants was found near the town of Tepexpan. The discovery was made after workers digging a ditch

*A Mayan mural from Bonampak shows a leader wearing a jaguar skin.*

*A Toltec terracotta figurine shown wearing a jaguar skin cloak.*

found mammoth bones. Archaeologists believed this site to lie on the great north–south migratory routes used by early nomadic hunters. They searched the area and discovered the Tepexpan Man, who breathed his last about 10,000 years ago.

Also known as the Elephant Man, Tepexpan Man and others like him were hunters of big game. They pursued herds in groups, following the animals' migratory routes. Later groups followed in the hunters' footsteps, tracking smaller game and finding nourishment from seeds and wild plants. These were the first hunter-gatherers to enter the region, whose descendants later settled as agriculturists.

During the Archaic period, from about 5000 to 1500BC, the first clues of continuous human settlement emerged in the

*An Olmec standing stone from the jungles of Tabasco (right). The Olmecs were the first of Mesoamerica's great civilizations, and their sophisticated art and architecture provided a blueprint for those to follow.*

form of an agricultural-based society. Evidence of cultivation, stone tools and crude pottery, has been found in the Central Valley area. Little is known about Mexico's earliest people, but they did provide a fertile seeding bed for the great civilizations that were to follow.

The Toltecs, Maya, Mixtecs and the Aztecs are some of the many peoples to have subsequently inhabited this region. Each participated in and contributed to the Mesoamerican culture that forms the foundation of the Mexican nation.

The clues to the past left behind by Mexico's first inhabitants are difficult to fathom. Much has been obscured by the abrasion of time and the chauvinism of colonialism. What remains are the ruins of vast cities that were, in some cases, larger than any to be found in Europe at the time that they prospered.

Perhaps most tantalizing of such clues to the past is the written record left by the Maya. Their writing system was, in its time, one of only five in the world. Historians and linguists are still grappling to decipher this little-understood voice from the past.

## THE OLMECS

The Olmecs were the first of these great civilizations. They emerged during the Pre-Classic era, around 1500BC to 300AD, and are believed to be the inventors of much that would define later Mesoamerican cultures.

Little is known about the inhabitants of the great Olmec cities that flourished in the jungles of Veracruz and Tabasco. For their influence over the cultures that would follow them they are regarded as the founders of Mesoamerican culture. They invented the first calendar and developed a hieroglyphic writing system. Theirs was a religion-based society that worshipped the jaguar god and made use of human sacrifice. Elements of this religion spread through much of central and southern Mexico. Their monumental architecture, the pyramids and plazas they created, were also adopted by cultures in the centuries to come.

The Olmecs rose out of simple beginnings in fertile coastal lowlands along the Gulf Coast. Ecologically, they were aided by an abundance of natural resources not enjoyed by the majority of

*This giant 2.5m-high (8ft-) Olmec head, carved from stone and weighing more than 20 tons, is thought to represent the visage of an Olmec ruler.*

This task would have required a large and disciplined workforce, which is further evidence of a hierarchical and well-organized society.

It is believed that Olmec society was controlled by strong rulers, at the head of a royal lineage, and it is speculated that the huge sculptures are portraits of these rulers. Many of these sculptured heads were found in regional capitals where it is assumed the rulers lived.

The Olmecs established intensive regional trade and nurtured talented craftspeople who produced an array of fine products. Archaeological digs have revealed Olmec stonework, such as magnetite mirrors and beads, in distant corners of the Mesoamerican region. Another major export of the Olmecs, and one that would have a lasting effect on the area, was their culture and religion.

The Olmec belief system was dominated by supernatural beings endowed with animal attributes. Jaguars, crocodiles, snakes and sharks were the most commonly revered animals and were often depicted in Olmec artwork. The Olmecs believed that humans could be transformed into special creatures strengthened by extraordinary animal qualities. Priests and rulers, the highest level of Olmec society, were given the attributes of the jaguar to symbolize their position and power.

Archaeological work continues in the Gulf Coast region, but despite attempts to solve the riddles of the past the history of the Olmecs, and more importantly their culture and religious beliefs, remain elusive.

One of the key problems yet to be resolved is the reason for the decline of the Olmec civilization. Excavations of three of the pivotal capitals or regional centres show that it existed for around 1200 years. The last major Olmec capital, known as La Venta, seems to have been mysteriously abandoned about 2400 years ago, by which time San Lorenzo had already been abandoned. Tres Zapotes survived these cities, passing Olmec influences on to the early Maya.

Mesoamerican peoples. Their agriculture was based on a combination of beans, corn, squash and the use of natural products found in the jungles of the area. In addition, the abundance of water in this fertile region made it easier for the Olmecs to flourish.

Today we can only speculate on the actual proportions of the Olmec civilization. However, aspects of their culture, such as their monumental works of art, have survived. The Olmecs used a powerful yet simple mode of artistic expression in the form of colossal heads that were chiselled out of monolithic volcanic rock. What is remarkable about these stone sculptures, some of which weigh up to 20 tons, is that the basaltic rock used in their construction was brought in from quarries up to 90km (55 miles) away.

*The Maya developed an advanced society that encouraged the building of impressive cities like Palenque* (above), *lined with elaborate pyramidal temples, towers and palaces.*

*A Mayan nobleman in all his finery. Note his fashionably sloped forehead.*

## THE MAYA

The origins of the Maya are a mystery, the demise of their civilization a riddle. They prospered in the lowland jungles of southern Mexico and neighbouring countries, leaving behind vast cities which at their height supported tens of thousands of people. The Maya were the longest lasting of the Mesoamerican civilizations. During a period of around 35 centuries, from 2000BC to 1500AD, they built elaborate temples and sprawling cities across southern Mexico and neighbouring territories. The inhabitants of these cities achieved incredible cultural and scientific heights during the Classic period of Mesoamerican civilizations (AD 300–900). However, about 1000 years ago, the Maya abandoned their cities and their civilization and retreated into the forests.

The achievements of the Maya are remarkable. They developed a complicated writing system and independently discovered the mathematical concept of zero. They were dubbed the 'Greeks of Mesoamerica' for their knowledge of science, the 'Romans' because of their well-drained roads, and the 'Egyptians' because of their pyramidal temples. At a time when Europe was still wrapped in its dark ages, the Maya developed an astronomically-based calendar. They calculated the length of the year to be 365.2420 days. The calendar we use today, the corrected Gregorian calendar, gives us a year of 365.2425 days. The Mayan's calculations were two ten-thousandths of a day short. Those used in the corrected Gregorian calendar are three ten-thousandths of a day too long. The Maya managed to get closer to a true year than we have.

They plotted the movements of the celestial bodies with an incomparable accuracy, correctly predicting both solar and lunar eclipses as well as the length of the year for Venus to within an error of only one day in every 6000 years. This apparent obsession with the movements of the planets and stars can in part be explained by the importance they attributed to the celestial bodies. The star we know as Venus was a god for the Mayan people.

The Maya were prolific writers. When they developed their hieroglyphic writing system it became one of only five writing systems in the world. Only a handful of codices (Mayan books) survived the Spanish Conquest. The rest – in which may have been an explanation and a record of an advanced culture – were destroyed by overzealous Spanish priests. Diego de Landa, the first bishop of the Yucatán, collected hundreds of Mayan books and publicly burnt them in the hope of erasing the Mayan religion. The secrets of this civilization are now written in stone on the walls of the remaining ruins. Obscured by time and half-hidden by determined forests, the temples only became the subject of serious research in the latter half of the 20th century.

As attempts to decipher the remaining Mayan texts and glyphs are progressing, more of the Maya culture is beginning to be understood. But much of what is 'known' is mostly speculation. It is believed that many of the Mayan temples were giant timepieces used to plot out the complicated Mayan calendar. Priests used the equinoxes and monitored the movements of the stars and planets to predict the seasons. This was a necessity in an area such as the Yucatán where there is very little ground water besides subterranean reservoirs, or *cenotes*. Therefore the Maya's survival relied on correctly predicting the seasonal rains for their crops.

A stone ring from a Mayan ball court (far left). The rules of this game are not fully understood, but it is believed that in many cases players from the losing team were selected to be sacrificed after the game.

The Temple of the Warriors (left) at Chichén Itzá. The great Mayan city shows many Toltec influences, and this temple is a larger version of the Temple of the Morning Star at the Toltec capital of Tollán. In the foreground is a serpent column, with its head on the ground and tail in the air. The tail formerly supported the roof.

The priests, as timekeepers, interpreted the patterns of time and space, and plotted almanacs around which the Mayan culture evolved. They developed an acute understanding of these patterns and used ritual to try to control the powerful energies released by the universe. Their complicated calendar runs on 260-day cycles that rotate within successive ages. The ending of the next age – with dire consequences – is predicted to be Sunday 23 December, 2011.

The Mayan pyramids were also places of worship. In the Mayan world blood was the concrete that bound the universe together. According to their mythology the universe and the people who inhabit it were created from the blood of their Creator. In turn, Mayan royalty spilt their own blood by piercing their lips and genitalia for the benefit of the gods. In return for the royal blood, considered to be the most powerful of all substances, the world continued, the sun rose and corn grew.

Other fragments of Mayan culture remain, such as a barely understood ball game in which two teams pitted themselves against each other using a solid rubber ball roughly the size of a football. Various Mayan sites have elaborate ball courts that seem to have played a central role in their lives.

## THE TOLTECS

In around 900AD northern warriors known as the Toltecs conquered the Central Valley. They built the magnificent city of Tollán near what is now the town of Tula de Allende. Theirs was a warrior society and the prototype for the militaristic Aztec empire.

Legend has it that a Toltec leader called Topiltzin encouraged the peaceful cult of the god Quetzalcóatl, and as the priest king, took on the god's name.

He was later defeated by a warlike faction led by his nemesis Tezcatlipoca (Smoking Mirror), and fled south to Cholula. After an influential stay he moved down to the Yucatán Peninsula, bringing with him the cult of Quetzalcóatl and other aspects of Toltec culture. The Mayan name for Quetzalcóatl is Kukulkán, the Feathered Serpent.

In 1168 Tollán fell to another wave of northern warriors, the Chichimecs. The last of these were the Aztecs.

Four great basalt warriors known as the Atlantes stand mute amid the ruins of columns atop the great Pyramid of the Morning Star, the focus of the Toltec city of Tollán.

## THE AZTECS

While the sun was setting on the Mayan civilizations of southern Mexico, a number of civilizations were taking root in the fertile Central Valley. Many of these early settlers were nomads from the arid northern areas who invaded southern settlements and were in turn displaced by later invasions. Among the last to arrive were the Aztecs who would be remembered as the last of the great classic civilizations of Mexico. They came from a mysterious region called Aztlán and brought with them their terrifying god Huitzilopochtli who granted them, they believed, prosperity in return for human sacrifice.

The Aztecs settled in the Central Valley around 800 years ago. Initially they served as mercenaries and vassals to the established rulers of the area such as Cozcoxtli, chieftain of the Culhuacán city-state. With time they grew in strength and established their own city at a site chosen by Huitzilopochtli, their all-providing god. The Aztec capital was founded as the realization of Huitzilopochtli's prophesy: the god wanted a city built at a place where an eagle was seen devouring a snake on a cactus which had taken root on a rock in a lake. Such was the beginning, in 1345, of Tenochtitlán, which means 'place of the cactus'. This city would eventually become the great sprawl that today is México City.

By all accounts the Aztec capital was an incredible city. Built on an island in a great lake, it was connected to the mainland by causeways. The lake provided an abundance of fresh water, was used for transporting goods and was a good source of food. The Aztecs used the lake to grow crops by placing nutrient-rich soil from the lake bed on wooden frames that became floating gardens. On these *chinampas*, as they were known, Aztec farmers planted corn, peppers, beans and squash, the essential diet of the Mesoamerican region.

The Aztecs ruled by way of a strict hierarchy. The head of the state was answerable only to Huitzilopochtli. The ruler's word was absolute and he was treated as a demigod. Supporting the ruler was a noble class, a form of absolute government who saw to the matters of state and were, in turn, rewarded with great wealth and power. The nobility shared an equal status with the priests who were the representatives of the gods, the overseers of religious ritual, writing, medicine and astronomy. Then came the merchants, the traders, the artisans and other ordinary citizens. The lowest level was that of the slaves, who were either prisoners caught in battle, awaiting their sacrificial death, or people who had voluntarily gone into slavery to pay off some debt or to survive a failed crop.

The Aztecs prospered and gained dominance of the Central Valley. Under the reign of the emperor Moctezuma I, the empire spread and even the wall-like mountains of the Central Valley could not contain his power. The warlike state embarked on far-reaching military campaigns that extended the empire as far

*The famous Stone of the Sun, also known as the Aztec Calendar Stone (although it is not a calendar), was unearthed in 1790 by workers digging on the edge of the main square, or zócalo, in México City. The stone shows the Fifth Age of humankind.*

*Human sacrifice, from an Aztec codex. The heart is removed and offered to the gods.*

*The foundation myth of Tenochtitlán, with the eagle devouring a snake on a cactus.*

*The Aztec ruler Moctezuma II, who was in power when the Spanish arrived in 1519.*

escape the wrath of a rival god, but who had vowed to return one day.

The 'strange creatures' who had appeared on the eastern fringes of the Aztec empire were the Spanish Conquistadors, come to claim the New World, as they called it. The small armada, led by the astoundingly ambitious Hernán Cortés, would forever change the face of Mexico, bringing to an end the Classic period of Mesoamerican history.

It was not just the Aztecs who were affected by the arrival of the Spanish. It has been estimated that there were around 25 million Indians living in the region at the time of the Spanish arrival. Within a century there were only an estimated three million left. The rest had been killed in battle or wiped out by the introduction of diseases to which they had no resistance, like smallpox.

## THE CONQUISTADORS

It is difficult to believe that so few could do so much. The Spanish Conquistadors landed on the coast of Mexico on a distant Good Friday in 1519, at a place

*Hernán Cortés, leader of the Conquistadors and first viceroy of New Spain.*

they named Veracruz (True Cross). The group of desperadoes were led by Hernán Cortés, a young Spaniard of limited military experience who possessed an audacious ambition, a sense of cunning and, perhaps, an inordinate amount of luck. With around 550 men,

south as Oaxaca and as far east as Veracruz. This expansion brought great wealth to the kingdom by way of tribute, and more humans for sacrifice to bloodthirsty Huitzilopochtli.

At the centre of Tenochtitlán was the Great Pyramid of Huitzilopochtli, where a steady supply of human hearts was plucked from living victims and offered to the god. As for the Maya, human blood was the cement binding the Aztecs' universe. Huitzilopochtli was the war god as well as the sun god, and the Aztecs believed that human sacrifices ensured their continued success in battle as well as the rising of the sun each day and the continuation of the universe.

The number of these sacrifices is beyond comprehension. When Ahuítzotl succeeded Moctezuma I, he is said to have celebrated his coronation with the sacrifice of 20,000 victims, most of them prisoners captured in battle. Some accounts claim that priests worked in shifts for four days in order to complete the gruesome task. However, many of these accounts were written by the Spanish and were used as justifications for the conquest, so their validity is often questionable.

Whether the work of Huitzilopochtli or not, the Aztec empire grew dramatically during the reign of Moctezuma II, who succeeded Ahuítzotl. At its peak the Aztec empire covered more than 150,000 km² (57,900 sq. miles).

At the beginning of the 16th century a comet lit the sky bringing with it, according to the Aztecs, a message of great change and portents of doom. Soon after, in 1519, a messenger arrived from the east coast with the news of a strange sighting. Tall, floating cities had been seen on the sea. These cities were inhabited by a strange kind of man, paleskinned and bearded. They carried with them dreadful weapons that spouted fire and were themselves immune to arrows. The creatures bore a remarkable resemblance to Quetzalcóatl, the god of the morning star, who according to Mesoamerican mythology had fled east to

*Illustration of Spanish Conquistadors and Indians, with Malinche translating for Cortés.*

Cortés also used the fractured politics of the region to his best advantage. For several centuries the warlike Aztecs had held cruel sway over much of what is

*A mask of La Malinche, 'the Traitor'.*

16 horses, 14 cannon and a handful of dogs, Cortés went on to conquer one of the world's greatest empires. In less than a year the Aztec empire would be destroyed, bringing to an end the age of the Mesoamericans and marking the beginning of the New World.

Ambassadors of Moctezuma II, the great Aztec ruler of central Mexico, met the Conquistadors. The feared ruler controlled a territory larger than Spain and ruled millions of people, but was totally unknown to the European powers. The Aztec ambassadors lavished the Spaniards with gifts. Huge gold calender discs the size of cartwheels, gold necklaces and a turquoise mask were among the treasures brought to the Spanish. Cortés had the gold melted down into ingots.

This was just the first hint of the many marvels that awaited the Spanish adventurers on their long journey to the Aztec capital. It was a journey that would take them past vast armies, in the course of which they would witness rituals that involved human sacrifice, and which

would lead them to a city larger than any seen in Spain.

Historians believe that one of the reasons Cortés was able to defeat the Aztecs was that Moctezuma II may have believed Cortés to be none other than the god Quetzalcóatl, who was believed to have fled to the east to escape a rival god but had vowed to return. It is surely one of the most amazing coincidences of history that Cortés arrived in Mesoamerica in the Aztec year *ce acatl*. The Aztecs had a cyclical conception of time, and according to their mythology, Quetzalcóatl would reappear in one of the cyclical returns of the year of his birth, the year they called *ce acatl*.

Further, Quetzalcóatl was fair-skinned and bearded. Moctezuma II did not know whether he should attack Cortés as an invader or worship him as a god. That the Spaniards rode horses, which were unknown to the Mesoamericans, and used terrifying cannons, contributed to their reputation as creatures other than humans.

today central Mexico. The Aztecs expected tribute from their subjects and demanded victims for human sacrifices from their enemies. On his march to the capital, Cortés took full advantage of his god-like reputation and made strategic allies with enemies of Moctezuma II. In this he was greatly aided by a young woman whom he received as a gift. She was a slave who spoke Náhuatl, an Aztec dialect, and also the Mayan language. The Spanish christened her Dona Marina, but she would be remembered in Mexico as Malinche, the traitor. Her abilities as a translator and her knowledge of the politics of the region were crucial to the Spaniard's success. Also assisting Cortés in this regard was Jerónimo de Aguilar, a Spaniard who had been shipwrecked off the Yucatán coast and who had learned the Mayan language. Thus Dona Marina translated from Náhuatl to Mayan, and Aguilar translated from Mayan to Spanish.

With these resources Cortés began his march to the Aztec capital. The Spaniards

*The Aztecs weeping after their defeat.*

had to avoid ambushes and fight battles along the way, but after three months they reached Tenochtitlán, where they were welcomed as gods. At various stages along the route Moctezuma II could have destroyed the Spaniards, but he ignored this advice from his councillors. His hesitation would prove to be fatal.

The Aztec capital they were welcomed into, built on its island and connected to the mainland by causeways, astonished the Spaniards. It was lined with handsome houses and great temples. When Cortés tried to describe the vast pyramid of Huitzilopochtli's Great Temple to the King of Spain, he wrote that it was of '...a size and significance no human tongue could explain'.

Matters came to a head soon after the Spaniards arrived. Using the killing of six Spaniards as an excuse, Cortés captured the Aztec ruler and placed him under arrest. This incredibly audacious act met with fierce resistance, and the Spaniards were attacked and driven out of the city. During their retreat they lost half of their number, but Cortés managed to regroup and retook the city ten months later. This time he won a comprehensive victory, aided greatly by the silent killer that had swept through the Aztec capital; Cortés and his men had brought smallpox into the world of the Mesoamericans. The Aztec capital was seized and a new rule was imposed on the land that was to become Mexico.

*A stucco portrayal of the genealogy of the family of Santo Domingo, compiled in the 17th century. At this time much of Mexico was controlled by a few elite families.*

## COLONIALISM

The Spanish were quick to exploit the great wealth of New Spain, as Mexico was known. Within six months of their conquest they had set about rebuilding the Aztec capital of Tenochtitlán, creating México City, the capital of New Spain. They built a cathedral near the temple of Huitzilopochtli, the feared god of the Aztec world who had been praised with the blood of thousands of human sacrifices. Nearby, Cortés had a palace built for himself where he, and successive viceroys, lived in great splendour.

The native peoples could do little to stop the disintegration of their world. The Aztec Empire was destroyed, the Spanish had killed its leaders and its people were dying from smallpox introduced by the Europeans. Churches were built on the sites of Aztec temples.

Over the next three centuries of Spanish rule, some 300,000 Spaniards settled in New Spain. They came in search of wealth and were rewarded for their loyalty to the crown with vast tracts of land and control over the Indians living on this land. The Spanish rule was not limited to the Central Valley. Within years the Spaniards had gained decisive control of the entire country, an area that stretched from the Gulf of Mexico to the Pacific, south into the Yucatán Peninsula and north into present-day Texas and California.

The Spanish ruthlessly imposed their religion onto the 25 million Indians living here, and attempted to obliterate their culture and beliefs. The society that evolved in this climate was based on a strict and clearly defined hierarchy. At the top were the *Peninsulares*, the

*Miguel Hidalgo, priest and revolutionary. In 1810 his cry of 'El Grito' began the struggle for Mexico's independence.*

Spanish ruling class who were the owners of the land. Beneath this elite ruling class were the *Criollos*, Mexican-born Spaniards who were the merchants, teachers, officers and civil servants of New Spain, who could aspire to wealth but who were never really granted any political power. Below the *Criollos* were the *Mestizos*, of mixed blood, the descendants of Spanish and Indian parents. They were followed by the Indians, who provided what amounted to slave labour for the Spanish mines and farms (known as *haciendas*).

The gap in terms of wealth, privilege and power between these classes was great. By the end of the 18th century the population of New Spain was approaching six million people, about 58 per cent were Indians, 25 per cent were *Mestizos*, 17 per cent were *Criollos* and less than 0.25 per cent were *Peninsulares*. Practically all the wealth was in the hands of the *Peninsulares*, and the wealth of New Spain was formidable. By the end of the 18th century New Spain was producing half of the world's silver and was providing almost two-thirds of Spain's revenues.

New Spain was built on abuse and exploitation. The first cracks of discontent came neither from the disempowered Indian masses nor the rejected *Mestizos*. It was the *Criollos*, the priests, teachers and military officers who were well-to-do and educated, but politically powerless, who were the first to lash out at the rulers of New Spain.

## INDEPENDENCE

In 1808 Napoleon Bonaparte invaded Spain and in doing so gave the *Criollos* a historical opportunity to overthrow the Spanish rulers of Mexico. Miguel Hidalgo y Costilla, a middle-aged priest inspired by the revolutions in France and the USA, began plotting his own revolution. By 1810 Hidalgo was preparing for an armed uprising, but word reached royalists who attempted to arrest him. Hidalgo rang the bell of his church and summoned his parishioners, not to a service, but to a revolution. With the cry of 'Death to bad government', Hidalgo lead his Indian parishioners, armed with sticks and machetes, against the royalists. This impromptu army was quickly joined by a host of New Spain's discontented, and swelled to an unruly mass numbering up to 80,000 people who

*Benito Juárez, a Zapotec Indian who became a respected ruler of Mexico.*

went on the rampage, massacring soldiers and civilians alike. In the town of Guanajuato alone they killed about 2500 people.

So began the struggle for independence that would last 11 years and claim over 600,000 lives. Independence was finally won by a *Criollo* by the name of Augustín de Iturbide, but little changed in terms of the social structure. Rich *Criollos* got richer by seizing land abandoned by the *Peninsulares*. Three hundred years of colonial rule had done little to prepare the country for a rational independence. Within seven months de Iturbide was overthrown and so began an era of great social and political instability for which Mexico would pay dearly.

During the next 30 years the government changed hands 40 times. The cost, not only in human lives, was immense. A weakened Mexico lost much of its north. In signing the Treaty of Guadalupe-Hidalgo, Mexico gave away what are now the states of Texas, New Mexico, Arizona, California, Colorado, Utah and Nevada for a paltry US$28 million.

Stability and reform eventually returned to Mexico. The bearer of some kind of calm for the ravaged country was a full-blooded Zapotec Indian named Benito Juárez. Growing up as an orphan on a *Criollo*-owned *hacienda*, Juárez managed to gain an education from a Franciscan priest. In a remarkable achievement Juárez went on to study law and politics and became Minister of Justice in México City, he helped draft the liberal constitution of 1857, and was named by the liberals as Mexico's president. However, fighting broke out between the liberals and the conservatives and Juárez was forced out of the city. He finally returned after four years of fighting and took up the reigns of a battered and very poor Mexico. One of his first actions was to place a moratorium on all payment of foreign debts.

Angered by this move, Emperor Napoleon III of France launched an attack on Mexico, ousted Juárez and placed Ferdinand Josef Maximilian on

*Porfirio Díaz ruled Mexico with an iron fist for 35 years before being forced into exile.*

the throne. Maximilian's position as a usurper and an outsider was untenable from the start and his short reign ended in 1866 with his execution. The presidency went back to Juárez who brought a well-needed dose of stability to the country during his 15-year rule. His successor, Sebastián Lerdo de Tejada, did not enjoy the same success. He was overthrown in 1876 by Porfirio Díaz, who maintained an iron-fisted rule over Mexico for the next three decades.

The strong-arm tactics employed by Díaz proved to be good for Mexico, after half a century of upheaval. Díaz brought peace to the country, eventually balanced the budget and paid off much of Mexico's foreign debt. When Díaz took office, Mexico had only 600km (372 miles) of railway, but by the end of his rule in 1911 the country had extended the railway network to 25,000km (25,530 miles) of track.

### REVOLUTION

Díaz may have conjured up an impressive economy, but he did so at the expense of the Indian population. His government allowed vast tracts of land

to remain or fall into the hands of the elite, much of it taken from the Indians. By the end of his regime less than ten per cent of the Indian population owned land and most were perpetually in debt, bound by law to remain on estates if they owed any money to the *hacienda* landlords. It was a system that was open to abuse and one that perpetuated the inequalities of the past. It would only be a matter of time before Mexico once again felt the tremors of change.

This time the bearer of change was a privileged *Criollo*, a rancher and member of one of Mexico's wealthiest families. Francisco Indalecio Madero published a book in 1909 that put forward the seemingly innocuous idea that presidential tenure should be limited to one term. The book hit a nerve and sparked off much heated debate. For his efforts Madero was named the 'apostle of democracy' and was thrown in jail by Díaz. Madero escaped to Texas, declared himself to be Mexico's provisional president in exile, and took up arms against Díaz. Despite having promised to retire from politics, Díaz tried to engineer his re-election in 1910, but many Mexicans had had enough. So began Mexico's cruel revolution.

It was the bloodiest and most confused war to be fought in the country, one known for its share of death and disorder. For the next ten years Mexico experienced unprecedented bloodletting which brought to the fore hundreds of years of inequality and injustice.

Originally, the revolution was led by two very different characters. One was Madero, who fought a middle-class revolution for a change in politics. The other was Emiliano Zapata, a child of peasant farmers in Morelos State who became a selfless champion of the disenfranchised Indians. Zapata wanted economic change, land reform and universal suffrage – a tall order for a country built on massive inequality. Other leaders and groups subsequently joined the fray, adding more confusion and in-fighting to the revolution.

*Emiliano Zapata, the revolutionary hero, fought for the land rights of the Indians.*

It could be said that Mexico's constitution was written in blood. One in eight Mexicans died during the revolution, which eventually resulted in the ratification of the liberal constitution that governs the country to this day. This constitution, drafted in 1917, embraced the ideals of the revolution. The constitution curtailed the power of the church, established state education, declared mineral wealth to be the property of the nation, and introduced a number of important social reforms. Land ownership was revised and a labour code was put in place.

## GOVERNMENT

As bloody as the revolution had been, it succeeded in binding Mexicans together into one nation, and ushered in a period of relative stability and prosperity.

In 1929 the Partido Revolucionario Institucional (PRI), or Institutional Revolutionary Party, came to power and has ruled Mexico ever since. With the demise of the Soviet Union, the PRI has the dubious honour of being the longest ruling party in the world today.

*A building in México City is lavishly decorated with the national colours and the freedom bell, symbol of Mexican Independence. Mexican politics has been dominated by the PRI (Institutional Revolutionary Party) for more than six decades.*

Although the PRI has enjoyed widespread support, it has also had to face sharp criticism in recent times. On 1 January 1994, an armed Indian group numbering between 1000 and 3000 people took control of four municipalities in the southern state of Chiapas. The group issued the Declaration of the Lacandōn Jungle and identified themselves with Emiliano Zapata, who fought for the land rights of peasants during the 1910–17 revolution. The Zapatistas, as they are known, have become a focal point in Mexico's political landscape. Led by a charismatic masked pipe-smoking spokesman known as Subcomandante Marcos, and inspired by eloquent demands for economic and social change, the group has won much support within the state of Chiapas.

Another blow came with the assassination of Luis Donaldo Colosio Murrieta. In 1994 the ruling party's presidential candidate was shot by a 23-year-old factory worker claiming to be working alone.

News that the Carlos Salinas de Gortari government had pocketed tens of millions of dollars between 1988 and 1994 pushed government confidence to an all-time low. Not helping matters was the onset of *La Crisis,* Mexico's economic crisis that has seen the peso devalue and interest rates soar.

Despite these criticisms and problems the PRI is seen as a pillar of strength in a region characterized by revolutions and political instability. During the 1940s the party had encouraged organized labour, accelerated land reform, nationalized a major part of the railway system and expelled foreign oil companies. Since the 1970s the expansion of Mexico's petroleum industry has stimulated the economy, but more recent falls in petroleum prices have hurt Mexico's growth.

## FOREIGN POLICY

Mexico's foreign policy has long been determined by its relationship with the USA. The dominance of this relationship in Mexico's economic activities is understandable. The countries share a 3117km-long (1937-mile) border, about 80 per cent of all visitors to Mexico come from the USA, and the USA is Mexico's biggest trading partner.

There are an estimated eight million Mexicans living in the USA. At least half of these are undocumented immigrant workers, aliens who have illegally crossed the border into the USA in search of better opportunities.

About 90 per cent of Mexican Americans live within the USA's four south western border states, namely California, Arizona, New Mexico and Texas. The obvious reason for this is their proximity to Mexico, but there are also historical reasons for this concentration.

When the Treaty of Guadalupe-Hidalgo was signed in 1848, it ended the war between the USA and Mexico at a severe price to Mexico. The treaty's terms saw half of Mexico fall into the hands of the USA. Mexico had little choice but to accept the terms and an estimated 75,000 Mexicans found themselves living within the USA. This community formed the foundation of the USA's Mexican population, which subsequently swelled with later waves of immigrants. These numbers have increased dramatically since the 1970s and it is estimated that nearly one-tenth of Mexico's people now live within the USA.

Despite the harsh terms of the treaty of Guadalupe-Hidalgo, the two countries' economic value to each other has smoothed out past resentments. Further, with 80 per cent of Mexico's population below the age of 40, the political scars of the past are little more than history-book memories. The youth are the driving force behind Mexico's emerging middle class and as such are well positioned to take advantage of the country's proximity to the USA. Aiding this process was the signing of the NAFTA agreement in 1994. The North American Free Trade Agreement aims to create a free trade zone between Mexico, Canada and the USA.

# ECONOMY

The events of the mid-1990s led to the devaluation of the peso. The move precipitated *La Crisis*, the country's worst recession in half a century. Interest rates shot up to 100 per cent and foreclosures ate away at middle class hopes.

The Crisis was stemmed by outside intervention and a stringent programme of economic adjustment. However, Mexico's gross domestic product shrank by 6.9 per cent. At present Mexico, as an emerging economy, continues to be buffeted by the global economy.

The economy is still struggling, but the characteristic Mexican optimism, abundance of resources available to this country and the tide of change should see Mexico through to better times. Mexico is Latin America's leading producer of oil and has the eighth-largest oil reserves in the world. In the past Mexico's economy leant heavily on this 'black gold', with bad effects during the 1970s oil crisis. When oil prices dropped, Mexico's economy tumbled.

The government is slowly moving towards a more balanced economy. More than 700,000 Mexicans work in *maquiladoras* or 'in-bounds', as they are known. These are tax-free assembly plants owned largely by foreign companies which manufacture an array of products. The in-bounds create jobs and it is hoped that they will bolster the country's manufacturing base. Mexico's proximity to the rich markets of the USA and Canada have made the country an attractive investment opportunity for international companies.

'Poor Mexico – so far from God, so close to the United States.' This Mexican proverb does much to describe the relationship between Mexico and the United States. This relationship has often turned sour but now much of Mexico's economic prosperity depends on goodwill between neighbours. Most of Mexico's visitors are from the USA. This figure represents a huge earning to Mexico in terms of tourism.

*The Pemex oil refinery at Tula. Oil is a driving force in the Mexican economy.*

The mushrooming resorts along the Pacific coast and areas of the Caribbean have added value to Mexico's tourism effort. The Pacific Ocean coastal resort of Puerto Vallarta attracts two million tourists a year, earning Mexico about US$300 million a year. With such resources at hand Mexico's prospects seem good.

However, Mexico's economy does face certain challenges. In Mexico corruption is part of an ingrained system known as the *mordida*, the 'bite'. The bite is everywhere, from the police officer who pockets a 50 peso note instead of issuing a ticket to corporate deals. Some argue that the *mordida* oils the economy, while others see it as the cause of many of Mexico's economic problems.

Many Mexicans are trapped in poverty. More than half of Mexico's wealth is owned by ten per cent of the population and more than half of Mexican families survive on less than 1000 pesos a month, about US$100. Mexico has a per capita income of $4000, compared to $25,800 earned by its US neighbours.

Average wages in Mexico are about US$5 a day, the equivalent of the hourly wage in the USA. Despite these grim figures Mexico's poverty is, in general, not overwhelmingly apparent. People seem to get by. Like the many colourfully painted clowns to be seen at busy intersections, offering a small show in return for a few pesos. Or the many food stallholders turning a small trade selling tacos and the like, seemingly happier in this occupation than begging.

This is not the first time Mexico has had to face problems, perhaps described by Mexicans as challenges. The country's history is a mosaic of rebellion, revolution and change. This is the motor that drives Mexico.

# PEOPLE

Mexico is home to around 95.8 million people. In 1960 the country had a population of about 35 million, and in the year 2050 the population is expected to grow to about 154 million. Mexico has a relatively high growth rate – at present the country's population is growing at about 2.3 per cent a year.

Cultural factors do much to explain Mexico's population profile. The family is a crucial unit within Mexican society and one that is greatly valued. The average Mexican family has 3.1 children.

Mexicans also live longer today than they did in the past, and the average person has a life expectancy of about 72 years. About 74 per cent of Mexicans live within urban areas. Large urban populations have concentrated considerable pressure on certain areas such as the greater México City metropolitan area which has a staggering population of about 20 million people.

### EARLY PEOPLES

Mexico's long history of settlement and invasion has created a culturally rich population. The earliest of Mexico's people were nomadic hunters who settled in the area so long ago that their existence

*Mexico is made up of a heady and sometimes volatile mix of Indian and European cultures. Cowboy hats, Western-style clothing and Indian cottons enliven this market.*

has slipped beyond even the memory of myth. From these early settlers rose the great Mesoamerican civilizations who developed their distinct cultures. The arrival of the Conquistadors led to the intermingling of Mesoamerican and European cultures which resulted in the formation of the Mexican nation.

Mexico today is predominantly a *Mestizo* nation; people of mixed Indian and Spanish descent. The country has three main ethnic divisions: *Mestizos* make up about 60 per cent of the population; about a third of the population is made up of full-blooded indigenous Indians; and about ten per cent of the country is made of a predominantly wealthy class of European ancestry.

### MESTIZOS

Mexico's people of Indian and Spanish blood are the most dominant group within Mexico. Their origins date back to the arrival of the Conquistadors and they represent the powerful synergy of these two cultures. Also absorbed within

the *Mestizos* nation were the estimated 150,000 Africans who were brought to New Spain during the early 1600s as slaves. The *Mestizos* mostly speak Spanish and are overwhelmingly followers of the Roman Catholic church.

### MEXICO'S INDIAN POPULATION

In 1870 the majority of Mexico's population was still pure-blooded Indian. However, the remaining 25 to 30 million Indians form a smaller, economically disempowered part of the population. Nowadays this population is concentrated in the Central Plateau (México, Hidalgo, Puebla), the south (Guerrero, Oaxaca, Chiapas) and in the east (the Yucatán Peninsula). About a quarter of the Indian population are believed to speak an Indian language and no Spanish. While not all of the 130 or so indigenous languages from Pre-Hispanic times have survived, some 82 identifiable Indian groups still speak their own languages.

The most prominent Indian groups include the Náhua, Otomi, Tarascan,

Huicholes, Tarahumara, Totonic, Huastec, Mixtec, Zapotec, Chinantec, Tzotzil Chol and Yucatán-Maya.

### SPANISH IMMIGRANTS

From the late 18th century until the 1950s Spanish immigrants made up the largest foreign group in Mexico.

During the first three centuries after the conquest about 300,000 Spaniards settled in the land they knew as New Spain. At the time of Mexico's independence this group was entirely in control of Mexico's political and economic power. The largest communities were in México City, Puebla, Veracruz and the Yucatán.

After Mexico gained independence Spaniards continued to settle within Mexico although they did not enjoy the special privileges that their forebears had enjoyed in the past. The prototypical Spanish immigrant was a young person, typically a male, lured from Spain to work for a relative or fellow countryman. He would work for this employee for a while and then start his own business, possibly a trading, transport or small-scale manufacturing business. With time the business might grow, and draw more immigrants to Mexico.

Mexico also became a refuge for people trying to avoid persecution in their home countries. With the decline of the Ottoman empire, the Lebanese community faced greater persecution in Europe and many of them opted to take their chances in Mexico and in other South American countries.

Other communities also came to Mexico to find a better life. Jewish emigrants experienced a freedom here that they had been denied in Europe. During the *Porfiriato* (1876–10), the 30-year regime of Porfirio Díaz, Mexico's immigrant populations grew with the encouragement of immigrant incentive schemes. The country's Jewish community also grew in numbers in the wake of persecution in Europe. By the 1950s there were about 24,000 Jews living in Mexico, and today there are around 35,000.

*The grand cathedral in San Miguel de Allende, in the colonial state of Guanajuato.*

*Tlahuizcalpantecutli, the Celestial Walker, one of the gods displaced by Christianity.*

# RELIGIONS

On the surface Mexico is a land of churches. The smallest towns will have some kind of church, while bigger cities invest their skylines with extravagant cathedrals. The churches and cathedrals are built within central areas in classical styles, usually around the plaza which is the living heart of any town or city. While shoe-shiners and food vendors gather around the plaza, people seek solace inside the churches.

The evidence of religion is overwhelming and surprising considering the difficult and sometimes controversial role the church has played in Mexico. During the conquest Catholic priests accompanied Hernán Cortés and the priests wasted little time in imposing their religion on the peoples of Mexico. The Spanish reacted savagely to the religions

of the Mesoamericans; idols were shattered, entire temples were torn down and the bricks used to build the prolific churches of New Spain. Priests were hung and the common people were forced to spit when the names of their gods were mentioned. Where the resistance from the Indians was more stubborn, the conquest was more brutal. The Maya, the last to hold out against the Spaniards, were forced into following the new god. Diego de Landa, the bishop of Mérida, burnt invaluable Mayan texts and in doing so obliterated the knowledge of centuries. Only a handful of Mayan books are known to have survived.

The Church of New Spain had much power, it owned vast tracts of land and was made rich by the tribute of a plundered nation. Priests were outside of the law and could only be tried by an ecclesiastical court. Perhaps due to the force

with which the Church laid its claim on Mexico, the religion soon took hold. A new god, one that did not demand human sacrifice, replaced the gods of the past – but an essence of the old religions remained within the new.

The Church had installed itself by force but it needed to inspire the faith of the Mesoamericans in order to find validity. In 1531 the required miracle happened. At a pagan site, formerly the temple of the Aztec earth goddess Tonantzín, an image of the Virgin Mother appeared to an Indian who had been converted to Christianity. Juan Diego, the seer of the miracle, had heard his name called out, and on turning he saw a dark-skinned Madonna. The vision asked that a church be built at the site of the Aztec temple, and so the Catholic icon replaced the Aztec earth-goddess. This vision was widely accepted throughout Mexico, and the Church found the legitimacy it was looking for. To this day Mexicans make pilgrimages to the basilica of the Virgin of Guadalupe in México City, and the anniversary of the miracle is widely celebrated on 12 December.

The prosperity the Church enjoyed at the expense of the ancient religions did not last. After Mexico's independence from Spain, the Church faced growing

*Serene angels outside a church in Colima State belie a legacy of religious conflict.*

criticism about its privileged position. Benito Juárez, Mexico's first and only full-blooded Indian president, passed laws to rein in the Church's power. In 1926, president Plutarco Elias Calles launched the most serious attack on the Church. Foreign-born clergy were deported, Catholic schools were closed, the clergy were forbidden to wear their robes in public, and in some areas priests were not allowed to perform their sacraments. Bands of militant Catholic guerrillas responded with attacks on government officials. The government responded to the militant *Cristeros*, as they were known, with force. *Cristeros* and priests were hunted down and shot or tortured, their bodies publicly displayed as warnings to others. Churches were destroyed and congregations were massacred.

What almost amounted to a war between the Church and State culminated in the death of President Obregón, who was assassinated in a restaurant by a Catholic follower. Eventually the conflict subsided, but the reconciliation has been a long and bitter process. Finally, in 1991, the Congress passed constitutional amendments that allowed members of the clergy to vote in elections, wear their habits in the street and run religious schools.

Despite the conflict between religion and the State, church groups flourished and today play an important part in the Mexican way of life. But there are also other religious or spiritual beliefs that are deeply embedded within Mexican daily life. These are the ancient workings of the *bruja* or *curandera*, the traditional healers who still make use of the ancient Mesoamerican knowledge. The *bruja* are generally seen as having supernatural powers, while the *curandera* make use of herbs for their remedies – although the line between the two often blurs.

The methods and practices of the *bruja* or *curandera* are widely used by Mexicans. Mayan traditional healers still use the ancient astrological beliefs and harness the power of herbs to treat patients. According to surveys conducted by the World Health Organisation, 85 per cent of Mexicans still use traditional medicines in some form. Many of these are administered by *bruja* or *curandera* who make remedies to cure anything from poor health to a broken heart.

It is difficult to know how seriously these practices are taken or how widely they are used, but judging by the abundance of practising *bruja* or *curandera*, it is clear that the wisdom of the ancients is very much alive in modern Mexico.

## FIESTAS AND CEREMONIES

Fiestas are the heartbeat of Mexico. Hardly a day goes by without a celebration or fiesta erupting in some part of the country. There are about 5000 to 6000 noted fiestas in Mexico each year. Some are national events, full of colour, ceremony and speeches. Others are regional events full of character and intricate ritual. All are accompanied by loud music and an abundance of food in the extravagant style Mexicans seem to love.

*El Día de los Muertos*, the Day Of The Dead, is one of Mexico's most popular and most interesting festivals. Although there are regional differences in how the festival is celebrated, it is generally

*An altar with a skeleton as part of the celebrations on the Day of the Dead.*

*A street artist's depiction of the Virgin of Guadalupe, a Mexican saint.*

believed that the souls of the dead swoop down on Mexico during the first two days of November. The dead seek out their loved ones and demand to be fed with their favourite snacks. On the night before the Day of the Dead, the smell of incense and the smoke of melted candles forms a heady aroma around the cemeteries of Mexico.

Families take to the graveyards where their departed have been buried and set up camp around the gravestones. Candles are burnt to light the way for the dead, who come to take their fill on

*Dancers performing in Aztec costumes in México City. The performances are also assertions of culture for many of Mexico's Indians.*

the abundant offerings. Favourite foods, cigarettes, beer, and personal belongings of the deceased are all included in the offerings. The graves are strewn with Cempasúchil flowers, the remnants of an ancient Mesoamerican practice.

The Festival of the Dead clearly reveals the synergy between indigenous Indian and European religions. Death has always played an important role in the belief systems of Mesoamerican peoples. Those who died had to pass through nine underworlds, each fraught with danger and impossible obstacles. Mictlantecuhtli ruled over this realm as the awesome Lord of the Dead.

If the dead succeeded in passing the obstacles they would reach a cave, the same cave from which people were born. In this way death was linked to life. Death was an abstract continuation of life and was celebrated rather than feared. Death, in the form of human sacrifices, was believed to be essential for the

continuation of the universe. The ancient gods had spilled their blood to create the world of people, and in turn people spilled their blood to ensure the continuation of the universe.

The colonial period brought a new perspective to beliefs about death, with the imposition of a vastly different religion. Now heaven and hell ruled the afterlife and good and evil became the condition of the living. The colonialists went to great lengths to graft their beliefs onto those of the Mesoamericans. Capitalizing on the belief that certain places had a special significance as gateways to other realms, or as places where gods dwell, the Church often tore down Mesoamerican temples and replaced them with churches.

The Catholic Church chose the first two days of November to honour the dead as All Saints Day, imposing the festival onto a Mesoamerican fertility festival that marked the time of the year

when the harvest was brought in. The ancient ceremonies also made use of offerings of Cempasúchil flowers. In this way two very different ritual traditions merged into one that has survived through the centuries as a powerful mix of pagan and Catholic symbols.

Today, during the month of November, death is everywhere in Mexico. In bakeries and sweetshops rows of sugary skulls resemble those chiselled into the ruins of ancient temples, believed to represent the sacrificial dead. The sugary skulls are eaten by eager children or land up as offerings on the gravestones of the dead. Death – depicted as a skeleton, and often flamboyantly dressed – stalks garishly across the country, appearing in newspapers and on advertising billboards. This comical skeletal figure, that is laughed at, respected and feared has walked across Mexico for centuries and shows no sign of tiring.

# ARTS

For centuries art has played an important role in the cultures of Mexico. The mesmerizing, colossal heads of the Olmecs, dating back some 3000 years, provide obscure clues as to the role that art may have played in that society. The immense effort required to transport the enormous boulders from which these heads were made suggests that the stone sculptures had a value beyond their aesthetic beauty; art and ritual were closely linked.

The Olmecs were not alone in this ritual use of art. The Maya chiselled incredible codes onto the walls of their temples. The glyphs, as they are known, were the syntax of the Mayan writing system, and their artistic beauty cannot be denied. The Maya also created statues and described their history in detailed murals. The Aztecs produced murals describing significant events and created elaborate sculptures to fill their temples.

There was more – archaeological evidence suggests that in every Pre-Hispanic society, art was practised in some way or other. Small pottery figures, less than 30cm (1ft) high, have been found in various sites around Mexico's central valley. Little is known about the origin or meaning. At Tlatilco, where some of the best examples of these statues have been found, figures can be seen dancing or playing music. Some had two heads or profiles with three eyes, strange prophets to the Cubist movement of Picasso and Braque.

The evolution of Mesoamerican art was brought to an abrupt halt by the arrival of the Spanish Conquistadors who declared the ancient world to be the New Spain and introduced a dramatic new aesthetic to the people of Mexico. The incredible colonial architecture that the Spanish left behind is no less beautiful than the art of Mesoamericans, but it was drastically different. It would take centuries of assimilation before the art of these two cultures could come to terms with one another.

*Mural of Miguel Hidalgo, the priest who began Mexico's struggle for independence. The work, by José Clemente Orozco, is in the government palace in Guadalajara.*

The period known as Mexico's artistic renaissance occurred shortly after the revolution of 1910. It was a time of great ideals that were supported by the residual anger of the revolution. Many of the conventions of the past were re-evalued and rejected. It was the perfect climate for the emergence of a groundbreaking art movement.

During this time Mexico's visual artists made an attempt to see and express a truer Mexico with an authentic voice. Artists revisited the wealth of Mexico's artistic past; sculptors studied the ancient works in stone and clay, while painters pored over the murals and drawings left behind by Mexico's first peoples. Artists developed a romance for all things pre-Hispanic and yearned to create an art form that had not been influenced by the shock of the Spanish arrival.

The Muralists came closest to answering this yearning. They were led by three flamboyant characters; Diego Rivera, David Alfaro Siqueiros and José Clemente Orozco. The 'Big Three', as they were known, were to characterize the Golden Age of Mexican art. 'The highest form of painting, the purest, the strongest, is the mural,' declared Orozco. 'It cannot be turned into an object for personal profit; it cannot be hidden for the benefit of the privileged few. It is for the people. It is for all.' These words define the aims and passion of the movement that inspired muralists to cover the walls of major public institutions with murals tackling historical and social issues.

Diego Rivera is perhaps the best known of the muralists. His prolific and sometimes controversial works can be seen in many buildings throughout Mêxico City. Using a pure fresco technique of hand-ground pigments painted on freshly laid plaster, Rivera set about capturing the past in his works. His depictions of history, although controversial, were never bland. His sympathy for the disenfranchised Indian people was clear, as was his anger at the Spanish Conquistadors whom he often portrayed as evil creatures, more monster than human. On the other hand, Mexico's Indians were depicted by Rivera as heroic figures replete with bold brush strokes and warm, earthy colours (see pages 111 and 117).

*Portraits of Frida Kahlo adorn the walls of Diego Rivera's studio. The flamboyant Rivera and the tortured Kahlo provided Mexico with its most colourful artistic couple.*

*Mexico is blessed with a wealth of colonial architecture, such as the grand church of Valenciana in the historic town of Guanajuato.*

Another artist whose work was born out of the hurly-burly of this time was Frida Kahlo. At the age of 22 she married the 42-year-old Diego Rivera, and together they provided Mexico with its most colourful couple. Kahlo painted immensely personal portraits of herself, one for each year of her life. Through her portraits she expressed the pain, happiness and occasional ambivalence of her life. Kahlo spent most of her life in intense physical pain. In her early years she was involved in a bus accident which shattered her pelvis, causing lifelong damage. She died prematurely at the age of 44, but she left behind a considerable body of work that convincingly describes the life and times of an artist living in the Golden Age of Mexican art. Kahlo's home in México City has been turned into an art museum that offers a glimpse into this era.

## ARCHITECTURE

The visitor to Mexico can appreciate more than 3000 years of architecture. They can visit Olmec cities, once-mighty Teotihuacán and the great Mayan cities of the Yucatán. They can see grand colonial buildings in the silver cities, México City's modern Polyforum Siqueiros, and the great glass and steel towers of the capital city's Stock Exchange.

Mexico has around 11,000 archaeological sites, which hint at the cultural achievements of the Mesoamerican civilizations. The Mayan ruins at Palenque (see page 150), Uxmal (page 160), and Chichén Itzá (page 164), show an advanced style of architecture that made the most of limestone. This highly workable stone is abundant in the Yucatán where it is known as *cantera*. Aztec buildings (see page 116) benefited from a rock called *Tezontle*, meaning 'petrified hair' in the Náhuatl language. This volcanic rock is found in tones pink and brown.

The Spanish brought completely new architectural styles to Mexico, although their buildings would be much enhanced by the advanced decorative skills of the Mesoamericans.

The earliest Spanish buildings often took the form of fortified churches built on Indian sacred sites. These churches were built from the rubble of the Indian temple buildings which the Spaniards had torn down.

In the 16th century many buildings were built in the Plateresque style (see page 80), which literally means 'silversmith-like'. The ornamental stone masonry made use of scrolling and flower motifs. In the 17th century, Baroque architecture (see page 98) exerted considerable influence on Mexican styles. Mexican late-Baroque reached its most exuberant form with the Churrigueresque style. Here incredible detail is lavishly applied to façades and surfaces (see page 74).

Given New Spain's great wealth, abundance of cheap labour and good building materials, it is not surprising that the country has such an abundance of churches and colonial buildings. During the three centuries of colonial rule, Mexico's architectural expression knew no boundaries. What remains is a fascinating collection of architectural styles.

## LITERATURE

Although Mexico's literature begins with the writings of the Mesoamericans, few texts from this time have survived as most of Mexico's earliest writings were destroyed during the conquest.

What emerged from the conquest was a series of significant chronicles that described the historical events that took place. Of note was the Conquistador Bernal Díaz del Castillo's book, *True History of the Conquest of New Spain*.

On the whole, however, the literature of the colonial era was characterized by weak copies of European novels. Mexico's displaced literature was dominated by an overwhelming Spanish influence.

The revolution of 1910 brought about a parallel literary revolution and a gritty realism emerged in works about the country's poorest-of-poor and the bloody revolution itself. Authors such as Mariano Azuela (1873–1952) produced

*Juana Inés de la Cruz was one of Mexico's most important 17th-century poets. A nun, she wrote passionate love poetry.*

social critiques such as *Los de Abajo*, meaning 'Those from Below'.

Mexico's contemporary literature has been dominated by formidable figures such as Octavio Paz and Carlos Fuentes. Both these writers have combined their literary vocation with careers as diplomats and have chosen to write about

social issues confronting Mexico. Paz won the Nobel prize for literature in 1990 and has received world acclaim for his essay 'The Labyrinth of Solitude, The Other Mexico: Critique of the Pyramid', which he wrote after the 1968 Tlatelolco student massacre. At the time of the massacre Paz was Mexico's ambassador to India, a position he resigned from as a protest against the killings.

Carlos Fuentes has also visited social issues in his many fictional and critical writings. Through his style of magic realism his novels examine Mexico's values, history and society. In his novel *The Death of Artemio Cruz* (1962), Fuentes wrote about the last living hours of a dying man caught up in the Mexican revolution. This work and others have established Fuentes as a major international novelist.

## MUSIC

Elements of Mexican music predate the Spanish conquest, particularly the use of percussion instruments that traditionally accompany dances.

*Music is an ever-present accompaniment to Mexican life, from the Mariachi bands serenading passers-by to these village musicians taking part in a festival in the Yucatán.*

So important was music to the Aztecs that they had music houses called *cuica-callis*, where children from the age of 12 studied music. Some of the instruments from this time are still in use. Contemporary folk music makes use of early Mesoamerican roots and also borrows influences from Spanish music.

There are a great variety of musical forms within the general theme of Mexican folk music. Traditional songs and melodies all carry within them a strong sense of being for the musicians performing them. Their tunes and rhythms are lively and their lyrics are accessible. One form, called the *corrido*, acted as a means of communication before other forms of media were available.

Mariachi remains Mexico's best known musical expression. Mariachi bands vary in size but usually include violins, guitars, bass-guitars, trumpets and singers. Mariachis can best be described as wandering minstrels who play melodramatic odes to love, suffering, honour and death. Dressed in costumes inspired by cowboy and Spanish flamenco attire, they are always on the lookout for amorous couples to serenade.

# MEXICAN CUISINE

When people gather in Mexico there is always food, and where there is food there is music. The food is usually tacos, a soft flattened corn bread filled with tasty meats and spicy chillis. The accompanying music is usually Mariachi, Mexico's equally spicy music. But in Mexico there is an overwhelming variety of both food and music to choose from.

Mexico has made a generous contribution to the world's palate. For starters, it is the home of the chilli, that most travelled vegetable which has found a place in so many of the world's cuisines. Mexico has not forgotten to honour the chilli and it is available everywhere in a variety of forms.

Most commonly the chilli is prepared as a salsa, a sauce. This is usually a concoction of tomatoes, onions and chillis. As Mexicans take their chillis so seriously, there is no lack of imagination in how the chilli can be prepared. The most common kinds are the thin green serrano, the larger jalapeño, tree chillis and Havanan chillis. A delicious snack is the

*Chillis have become Mexico's best known contribution to world cuisine.*

poblano chilli stuffed with cheese and then deep fried.

Mexico's influence on world cuisine does not end with the chilli, however. Corn, beans, tomatoes, chocolate, avocados and vanilla are a few of the many foods that were first found in this region. Mexico does its abundance of natural ingredients proud and eating seems to be a national pastime in this country. Streets are littered with food stalls that sell Mexico's answer to fast food. The food is usually made on the spot with devastating speed. Tortilla-sellers usually turn a brisk trade – they need to in order to make a living. For next to nothing a tortilla – Mexico's most common snack – can be filled with anything tasty, a sprinkling of onion and a dash of herbs. Prepared in an instant, it is best eaten hot with a lick of chilli. There is a vast array of dishes to tempt the palate. The tamale, spiced corn bread steamed within corn leaves, is a popular dish. It is good served hot and washed down with some of Mexico's fine beer.

The Mexican palate does not stop at the hot stuff. Fruit plays a big part in the Mexican diet and fruit stalls are common. Known as *Surtido de frutas*, they serve refreshing fruit cocktails made from chunks of watermelon, papaya, pineapples, apples and any fruits in season.

*Mole Poblano, the most traditional Mexican Mole, which requires up to 30 ingredients, including indigenous Mexican spices and European imports such as garlic.*

Mexican bakeries also tempt with a fine array of breads, many of them sugary-sweet and delicious.

Not to be forgotten is tequila, Mexico's favourite drink. This head-splitting liquor is made from the fermented juice of the crushed pineapple-like base of Agave Cacti. The cactus is native to the state of Jalisco where the town called Tequila is still the centre of the country's million-dollar tequila industry. Mexico offers an overwhelming variety of tequilas – no two are the same, but one needs to develop a discerning palate to tell the difference. More mature tequila has a golden hue.

# CITIES

It is in **Tijuana** that the USA meets Mexico. Although this city is greatly influenced by its northern neighbour it has a distinctly Mexican atmosphere. Few of the American visitors who arrive overland from the north would describe Tijuana as beautiful, however. It has the feel of a town that grew up too fast.

The city itself is a clash of street signs, rising buildings and a crush of concrete housing. But within the fast-growing sprawl is a dynamic economy that is providing a few answers to Mexico's economic ills. *Maquiladoras*, tax-free assembly plants, often owned by foreign multinational corporations, employ hundreds of thousands of hard-working Mexicans, adding a vibrancy to this city. It is Mexico's city of opportunity, and Tijuana's population of about a million people is growing at a staggering 5 per cent a year.

**Monterrey**, another northern city, is said to have more character than the younger Tijuana. Here colonial cathedrals are dwarfed by high rise buildings, monuments to Mexico's modern economy. This open city, with its back to the Saddle Mountains (1800m; 5906ft), is growing steadily out into the surrounding desert-like landscape. The three million people who live here will need the leg-room. The city's proximity to the

*Guadalajara, the capital of Jalisco State in the central region of Mexico, is the country's second-largest city. This colonial city nevertheless retains a laid-back atmosphere.*

*The World Trade Centre and Polyforum Siqueiros show the changing face of México City.*

*Puebla has a reputation as a conservative town, which is reflected in its colonial architecture.*

The city of **Puebla** hovers between the past and the future. As a staging town between México City and the port city of Veracruz, Puebla grew rich on passing trade. During this time the city built a vast collection of colonial buildings that still remain as the heart of this city. As rich as the city's past was, however, Puebla is now very much caught up in the modern pace of Mexico, and is the country's fourth-largest city.

East of México City is **Veracruz**, the oldest of country's colonial cities. It was here that Hernán Cortés and his Conquistadors landed to lay claim to their New World. Since that first invasion, the city that faces the Gulf of Mexico has often been the first port of call for outsiders who have each added their traditions to the ways of this diverse place.

Now Veracruz has been made wealthy by Mexico's billion-dollar oil industry. Despite the raw energy that drives the city, there is however still a sense of the old world from which the city of the 'True Cross' arose.

**Oaxaca** is planted amongst the tumbling mountains of southern Mexico. Like so many of Mexico's cities, Oaxaca has a colonial heart. The plaza is dressed with towering cathedrals and open-air cafés which invite visitors to squander a few hours simply watching the passing of life. In Oaxaca it is a show that will not disappoint. Come sundown the shoeshiners and traders flogging colourful balloons retire. Then the plaza explodes with fireworks and colour as some festival or other gets under way.

**Mérida** is the largest of the Yucatán's cities. The city of almost one million people seems noticeably different to other parts of Mexico. It is where many of the region's remaining Maya live. Mérida thrived at the turn of the century as the centre of the world's fibre industry when large plantations of Henequén Cactus provided the raw product to make rope. Although the industry was crushed by the introduction of nylon fibres, a great number of grand buildings remain as reminders of more prosperous times.

USA and its business-minded approach has made it an important link in the economic chain that binds Mexico and its wealthier neighbour. Despite the growing economy, Monterrey has a spaciousness that is lacking in some of the country's other economic centres.

Further south is the grand city of **Guadalajara**, the crown of Mexico's colonial heartland. Guadalajara is Mexico's second-largest city and the capital of Jalisco State. Despite its size and official status it is a laid-back place. The hurly-burly of city life is softened by the countless colonial buildings and a sprawling plaza that is at the city's heart.

The head-turning architecture and the many plazas are gifts from the past, from a time when Guadalajara was the centre of the world's silver mining trade. Other industry has since taken the place of silver, but the city still maintains an air of wealth and beauty.

From the air **México City** is covered by a grey greasy cloud. The pollution from 20 million people seems to make it an unbearable city to live in, but beneath the clouds is a city that seldom fails to charm visitors who care to give it a chance. The chaotic pace of México City is at once exhausting, bewildering and intoxicating. Millions of cars rush along the main arteries that snake out from the centre. Some of these roads were once causeways linking the city of Tenochtitlán, the great Aztec island capital, to the mainland. Now clowns juggle for the cars stuck in the gridlock that often jams these ancient paths.

México City is a heady cocktail of indigenous Indian, colonial and cosmopolitan influences, a multilayered mixture of the old and the new. Taking it at face value, many people avoid Mexico's capital, but in doing so they fail to experience the essence of Mexico.

# MEXICO TODAY

There can be few places in the world like Mexico on a Sunday afternoon. Then families take to the streets, usually to the prolific plazas found in every town and city around the country. In Guadalajara, the main plaza fills with buskers, usually mime artists, who draw a circle of people around them as they perform, while bands play for a few pesos. Their stage is the colonial grandeur of this city.

In Mérida, the Yucatán's main city, Yucatecans gather in the old part of town. Here people revisit their past and perform traditional dances, or mariachi bands gather like gentle mobsters looking for amorous couples to serenade. In México City, Chapultepec Park is full on Sundays. The 690ha (1700-acre) park was once an island in a lake, visited by the tribes who went on to build their Aztec capital nearby. Now families gather here to avoid the concrete crush and bustle of México City.

Sunday is Mexico at its best. The week's irritations, the stumbling peso, the sting of the *mordidas*, the bite of corruption, are all pushed aside. At least for a day. Mexico's problems never lie too deeply beneath the surface, but they are often wrapped in the colourful lifestyle of the people. The thin disguise is convincing.

In the vocabulary of world economics Mexico is described as a developing nation. Some aspects of Mexico's economy are developing rapidly, but many of Mexico's people have been left behind. They are poor and the gap between those who have and those who do not is increasing. The ranks of the poor are mainly made up of Mexico's Indigenous Indians and swelling urban populations who find it difficult to find a place for themselves in the country's developing economy. As the millennium approaches Mexico faces a number of social, political and economic challenges.

When Cortés and his Conquistadors entered the valley of Mexico, it is written that Popocatépetl Volcano was erupting. The Aztecs saw the eruption as a smoky

*Popocatépetl Volcano, Mexico's second-highest peak, slowly erupts against a tranquil sunset.*

prophesy, a messenger of great change. The Conquistadors, who brought such profound change to this country, ignored the fuming mountain and went on to claim their prize, the Aztec capital, the heart of Mesoamerica.

Mexico today is a mix of the past and present: part Indian, part Spanish, but mostly something else that is unique. This diversity, shaped through painful turmoil, is the country's strength.

Popocatépetl is once again erupting, albeit quietly. Like the mounting heat trapped within the depths of this giant volcano, Mexico seems set for change. Who knows when that heat will erupt or what the outcome of Mexico's present situation will be. Whatever happens will be endured and overcome in a uniquely Mexican way – one that is nourished by family, by laughter and by Sunday afternoons.

# BAJA CALIFORNIA
## FROM TIJUANA
## TO CABO SAN LUCAS

Baja California Peninsula is a fortress of sea and rock, an inaccessible land that contains a wealth of undisturbed fauna and flora. Some of this changed in 1973 when Highway 1 was completed. The road that runs from the border city of Tijuana to Cabo San Lucas opened up the Peninsula to some extent. However, even today the sparsely populated Peninsula continues to resist human settlement and is known for its completely isolated beaches and pristine waters. The jagged mountains that dominate the Peninsula hide deserts and a harsh beauty that many visitors find irresistible. Tourism has become the Baja's largest cash crop and the Peninsula is a favourite destination for game fishing and diving.

At first glance the region's strange beauty is not obvious to the eye. Entering Mexico from the northwest you will find an inhospitable land characterized by a desert-like climate. Extreme temperatures here can swing from 50°C (122°F) to zero within 24 hours. For this reason the region has escaped some of the rapid development seen in other parts of Mexico. The Peninsula's salt works is one of the few industries to have taken root. However, some environmental groups are concerned that such development may damage the area's sensitive ecology.

Although this arid finger of land has a scanty rainfall of only around 250mm (10in) a year, it has attracted a multitude of creatures, many of them endemic to the area.

Gray Whales break their 20,000km-long (12,428-mile) migratory route between the icy northern Arctic waters and the Pacific Ocean at Scammon's Lagoon. Baja California Peninsula, site of the only known breeding grounds of the Gray Whale, has become the hub of a multimillion-dollar environmental tourism industry.

In the north, a number of towns have mushroomed along Mexico's 3117km-long (1940-mile) border with the USA, their growth spurred on by their proximity to the rich markets across the border. In the North West the town of Tijuana, with its million inhabitants, keeps pace with San Diego, its twin American city. Tijuana's growth rate is around five percent a year, making it one of Mexico's fastest-growing cities.

The border between Mexico and the USA is extremely porous and many Mexicans attempt to cross over to their wealthy neighbour. More than a million people are arrested each year in their quest to reach the USA.

Making good on those who don't cross the border are multinational companies who have established *maquiladoras* along the border. These vast assembly plants manufacture anything and everything from television sets to shoes and have become an economic force to be reckoned with.

Bilingual storefronts (above and bottom) *are common in the border town of Tijuana, a telling sign of the close ties between Mexico and the USA. English and Spanish are both spoken in this town at the interface of two countries. Tijuana (left), a town that is growing rapidly, spills over into an arid land. Like many of the cities within Mexico's northern border lands, Tijuana has pegged its economic successes on good relations with the USA.*

PREVIOUS PAGES:
PAGE 46: *Exploring Los Islotes in the Gulf of California.*
PAGE 47: *The Gray Whale migrates to the warm waters off the Baja California Peninsula to breed.*

*A tangle of street signs* (right) *clutters Tijuana's skyline. Many Mexicans visiting the main border town hope to cross over into the USA, some of them illegally. In 1995, for instance, 1.2 million people were apprehended trying to make the crossing.*

*Boomtown: banks and insurance houses* (below) *crowd Tijuana's business sector. Tijuana's economy is based on cross-border trade and tax-free assembly plants. It is a good mix – Tijuana enjoys annual growth rates of about five percent.*

An Organ Pipe Cactus (above) *rises above the Gulf of California. Also known as the Sweet Pitahaya for its sugary fruit, this cactus is one of the most important sources of food in the Peninsula. The Indians of Baja California enjoyed the fruit so much that they set their calendar by the Sweet Pitahaya's fruiting season, a time of abundance in this usually barren region. Cacti, such as these growing on the shores of the Gulf of California* (opposite), *are common throughout much of northern Mexico and form the largest floral group in the Baja California Peninsula. Of the 110 species found here, 60 are endemic.*

*The salt mines at Guerrero Negro* (left), *not far from Scammon's Lagoon on the west coast, are one of the few viable forms of industry that can be sustained on the Baja California Peninsula.*

Tourists from San Diego (above) *make their way to the world's only known Gray Whale breeding grounds. Almost 20,000 of the gentle leviathans migrate to the warm Pacific waters off the Baja California Peninsula each year. The whales settle in three of the Peninsula's coastal lagoons during winter after spending the summer months feeding off the nutrient-rich Arctic waters. Arriving in December, the Gray Whales give birth in January and February and begin their return trip to the Arctic in March, accompanied by their young.*

The mouth of the vast Scammon's Lagoon (right), midway along the west coast of the Peninsula, hides one of the three Gray Whale breeding grounds. The lagoon was hidden in this isolated part of the world by vast sand dunes until the whales were discovered by Charles Melville Scammon in the 19th century and were hunted almost to extinction. The Gray Whales also favour the nearby Laguna San Ignacio, and the lagoon at Bahía Magdalena further south along the Peninsula. More than 250,000 tourists a year make their way to this remote region to observe the whales, which have been protected by a whale sanctuary since 1972.

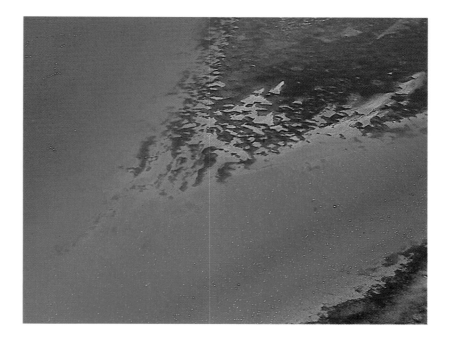

In recent years the waters off La Paz have become the favourite hunting
ground of big-game fishing enthusiasts. A number of resorts such as
Loreto and San José del Cabo have been developed to serve the needs of
fishing tourists. Of particular interest to big-game fishing are the Striped
Marlin found in this area – a recent specimen caught here is said to be
the largest in the world.

*A Green Turtle* (top) *and a Californian Sea Lion* (above) *enjoy the warm waters of the Pacific Ocean. These abundant waters were made famous by John Steinbeck who wrote about the pearl divers of La Paz in his novel* The Pearl. *The pearl hunters continue to dive the warm waters in search of pearls, but are now joined by large numbers of visitors who come in search of the area's living marine treasures.*

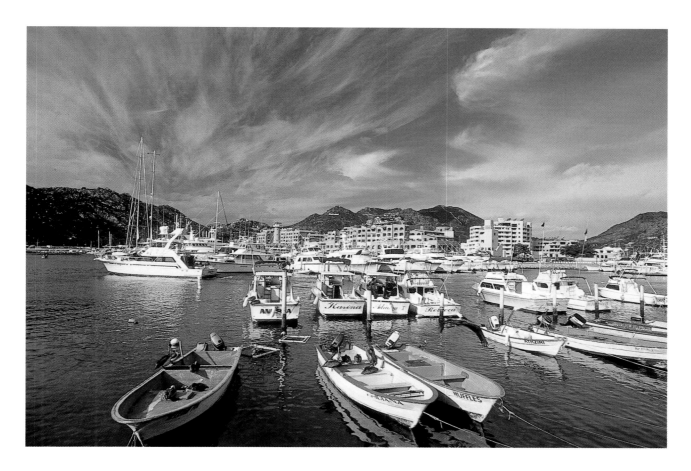

The laid-back town of Cabo San Lucas, which was little more than a fishing village 15 years ago, now exudes a sophisticated resort-like atmosphere (opposite top and bottom). A number of hotels and resorts have sprung up along the Pacific coast offering services aimed at tourists from the USA and elsewhere. The Baja California Peninsula offers good diving, game fishing, and surfing – with huge Pacific waves rolling in to break on beaches such as those of the renowned island of Todos Santos, off Ensenada in the northwest. Recreation at Cabo San Lucas includes a healthy diet of sun, sea and golf on four courses. The marina at Cabo San Lucas (above) draws a number of boats and yachts to this town, the most southerly on the Baja California Peninsula. To truly explore the Peninsula's 3400km (2111 miles) of coastline, water transport is recommended, as many of the Peninsula's beaches are only accessible by sea.

Cabo San Lucas is where the waters of the Gulf of California, once known as the Sea of Cortés, and the Pacific Ocean meet. The waters here are particularly rich in marine life and are popular with divers. This headland (right), known as El Arco (the Arch), marks the most southerly point of the 1260km-long (782-mile) Baja California Peninsula, which is the longest in the world.

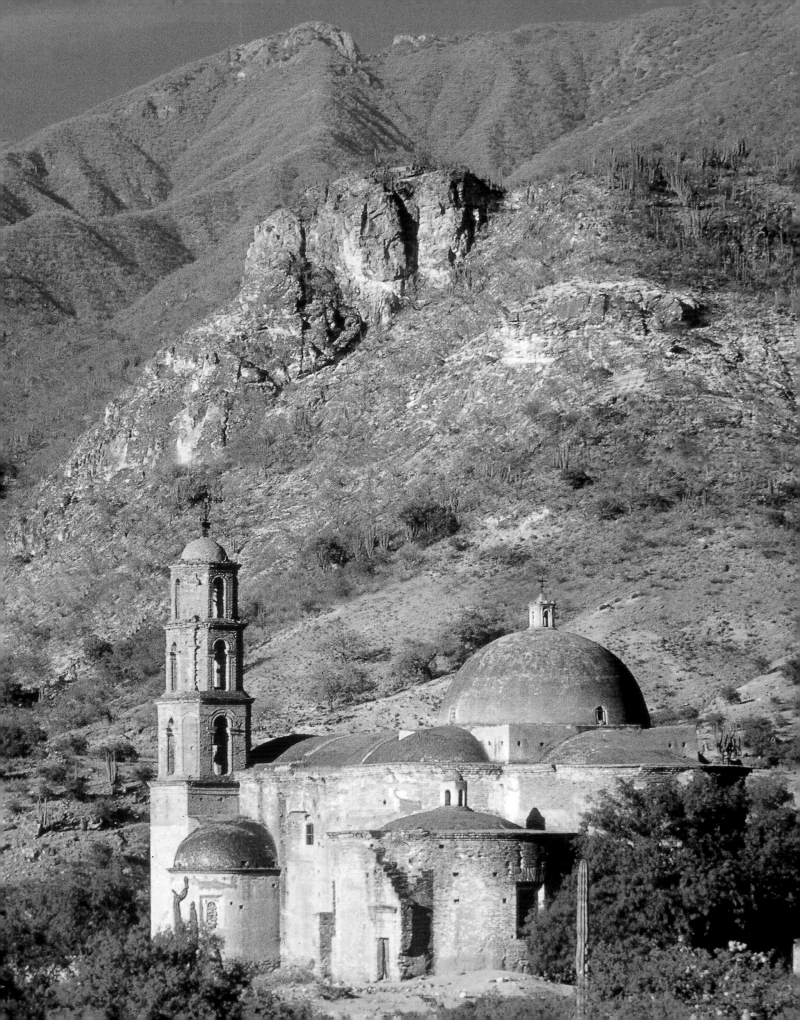

# THE ARID NORTH
## FROM THE DESERTS OF SONORA TO TAMAULIPAS

The north is the last refuge of the Mexican cowboy, a sparsely populated region with extensive grasslands ideal for cattle farming. Most of Mexico's wheat comes from this region. The state of Sonora, which runs from the USA border and down along the Pacific coast, is the country's biggest producer of wheat. The other major wheat-producing states are Sinaloa and Nayarit. Together, these three states account for around 20 per cent of the total area of Mexico, but are home to only six per cent of the country's population.

The once remote Sierra Madre Occidental, the backbone of Mexico, is being infiltrated by a network of roads and the modern world. The 1290km-long (800-mile) range is known for its vast canyons that dwarf the better known ones in the USA. The drastic geography has long been a barrier to the outside world and has been the last refuge of the reclusive Tarahumara Indians.

The Tarahumara, numbering about 60,000 people, were forced into the mountains by centuries of persecution. Today they still cling to their culture in the face of a changing world. The mountains have also traditionally provided a refuge of another kind. Renegades, including Pancho Villa, and drug smugglers have often sought out the maze-like canyons to hide in. Today the canyons hide opium poppies, used to make heroin, and marijuana fields. The economy of the region has, however, traditionally rested on timber production. Locals make use of the tropical forests that flank the Sierra and the highland stands of pine and oak. Unfortunately, due to excessive harvesting, only two per cent of the intact old growth now remains. Besides the woodlands the canyons hide an incredible array of wildlife, made diverse by the combination of high desert and forest areas. However, this is disappearing fast due to human pressure on the area. The grizzly bears that once thrived here are gone and the wolf population is dwindling.

Today tourism is seen to be the area's main hope. The train that runs between Chihuahua and Los Mochis is a big drawcard for tourists hoping to experience the mountains. Tourism may prove to be an elixir for the small lumber town of Creel. Up until now this frontier town has existed as a small outpost, an island of humanity within the vast Sierra Occidental. Now people visit Creel simply to see the mountains and enjoy the town's cowboy atmosphere. They can then retreat to seaside resorts such as Mazatlán and Sayulita on the east coast of the Gulf of California.

The north, one of Mexico's most sparsely populated areas, has a distinct character. This great arid region with its deserts, plains and mountain wildernesses is defined by a sense of timelessness and isolation.

PREVIOUS PAGES:
PAGE 58: *A solitary cathedral near the small town of Satevó, south of Chihuahua City, is a survivor from colonial times.*
PAGE 59: *A lone* vaquero, *or Mexican cowboy, rides the horizon in Chihuahua State, where vast grasslands feed a thriving cattle industry.*

*The Cerro Colorado* (above), *a sprawling volcanic crater, forms a scar along the Sierra del Pinacate mountains in the arid Sonora State. Here temperatures often rise to around 30°C (86°F). Sonora has long been a source of precious metals including gold, silver, copper and tin.*

*A Coyote* (top) *and a Mountain Lion, or Puma* (above), *from the great desert wilderness of Sonora State. The deceptively life-less landscape comes alive at dusk when the hardy desert creatures emerge from under rocks, from out of burrows in the sand and in the case of some woodpeckers and owls, from holes hollowed out of cacti.*

A Tarahumara woman's hand-made baskets (opposite top left) *tempt tourists riding the Copper Canyon train. The train runs between the highland city of Chihuahua and the coastal city of Los Mochis on the Gulf of California, passing through the land of the Tarahumara Indians* (opposite top right). *Centuries of persecution have forced the Tarahumara to seek refuge in the fortress-like canyons of the western Sierra Occidental. They eke out a living through hunting, selling their wares and subsistence farming of livestock and golden wheat* (opposite bottom). *Considered to be the most traditional of North America's Indians, many Tarahumara still observe practices such as their two- to three-day-long foot-races. Contestants may run nearly 200km (125 miles) in one race, sometimes kicking a wooden ball along in front of them as they go. They set great store by their athletic prowess, and refer to themselves as the Rarámuri, or 'Running People'.*

A dancer at a fiesta (right) *in the town of Cuauhtémoc celebrates the vibrant traditions of northern Mexico. Cuauhtémoc is named after the last free Aztec emperor, a cousin of Moctezuma II, and there is a large monument to him in the town. It is a major market centre for the Tarahumara Indians and also for the large Mennonite community (a Protestant Christian sect) which arrived in the 1920s and converted large tracts of barren land into bountiful farmland through irrigation.*

In times past the sleepy town of Creel (above) in the Sierra Tarahumara in Chihuahua State grew on the strength of the region's timber industry. Now small hotels have taken root in this high-altitude town which offers itself as the gateway to the Sierras. Visitors to the region break the 650km (400-mile) Copper Canyon train journey at Creel.

Cowboy boots (left) are for sale in Chihuahua where the cowboy way of life continues. The romantic image of the 19th-century American cowboy was based on Mexican vaqueros – the first cowboys – whose life in the saddle was adopted by Americans who headed out west. A sign in the town of Parral (opposite top) clearly lets visitors know that Mexico's north is cowboy country. Many of the cattle (opposite bottom) bred in northern Mexico are exported to the hungry markets of the USA.

A balancing pedestal rock (left) *is just one of the many bizarre rock forma-tions found in the majestic* barrancas, *or canyons, that line the Sierra Madre Occidental mountains, Mexico's most extensive mountain range. Some of these little-explored canyons, collec-tively known as the Barranca del Cobre, or Copper Canyon, are deeper than those of the more famous Grand Canyon in the USA, with the largest plummeting some 2000m (6562ft). A view* (below) *across the Copper Canyon shows a maze of mountains which have at various times offered sanctuary to Indians, revolutionaries, bandits and, in more recent times, drug dealers.*

A number of rivers drain off the Sierra Madre mountains (above), eroding great canyons out of the rock. Some Tarahumara Indians still seek refuge in caves in the lower parts of these canyons in the winter months. This Black Bear (right) is one of the few of its kind that remain in the remoter parts of the Copper Canyon, which are a sanctuary for a number of endangered species that include the Mexican Wolf and the Imperial Woodpecker. A programme has been introduced to bring back the Mexican Wolf, but human pressure – including activities such as logging and mining – still threaten the existence of wildlife in the area.

The carnival of Mazatlán (above) is said to be one of the best in the world, and is mentioned in the same breath as those held in Río de Janeiro and New Orleans. Each year for five days before Lent the town erupts as the carnival gets under way. Mazatlán is a popular resort town known for its beaches (left) and game fishing (below). The world renowned Mazatlán fishing competition is held each year at the end of August. Fishing is taken very seriously in this town, so much so that the bishop of the town leads a procession down to the docks each year to bless the fleet and mark the beginning of the fishing season. The procession is naturally accompanied by much celebration.

Coconut palms (below) *greet visitors to Sayulita in Nayarit State with visions of paradise. Set on the Pacific Coast, Sayulita is typical of many of the resort towns that lure visitors with their pristine beaches* (right) *and fair weather. In the 1970s most of the Pacific coastal resort towns were small fishing villages, remote and unknown. Now they play an important role in Mexico's tourism effort.*

Harvesting chillis in Durango State (opposite). The chilli (from the Spanish word chile, derived from the Náhuatl chilli) is one of Mexico's best known indigenous crops. After the Conquistadors were introduced to the chilli it did not take long for this fiery fruit to win favour throughout the world. Of the 200 varieties of chilli known to Mexico only a few are excessively hot. The Yucatán habanero and the serrano have earned themselves the honour of being Mexico's hottest. Visitors are advised to sample these with care.

An orange light adds colour and dramatic shadows to the incredible formations (above) found in one of the 16 illuminated caverns of the Grutas de Garcia, the Garcia Caves, in the state of Nuevo León. This is Mexico's biggest and most beautiful series of caves.

Lynx (right) comfort each other in Tamaulipas State. The few Lynx that survive in the wild are increasingly threatened by clashes with human development.

# COLONIAL HEARTLAND
## FROM GUANAJUATO
## TO VERACRUZ

The colonial heartland is the timeless Mexico. Here cities rich in colonial heritage seem to be snagged on a Sunday afternoon of several hundred years ago. Richly fertile and blessed – or cursed – with large deposits of silver, this mountainous area attracted Spaniards soon after their arrival in Mexico. There are numerous spectacular cities that remind

one of the wealth of this region. Guanajuato was for centuries the most affluent city in Mexico, and has been declared a UNESCO World Heritage zone to preserve its past.

To the east is Guadalajara, Mexico's second city and one that is also rich in colonial heritage. In this area the town of Tequila continues to produce the fiery Mexican drink of the same name. Tequila is made from the abundant fields of the Maguey Cactus that cover the land. A staggering 100 million litres of tequila is produced annually, accounting for three per cent of Mexico's gross domestic product.

Once across the invisible line of the Tropic of Cancer, the landscape of Mexico changes markedly. The land turns green and the climate softens. Scattered along an 800km (500-mile) stretch of coastline between Puerto Vallarta in Jalisco State and Punta Maldonada in southern Guerrero State lie some of Mexico's best known resorts. Puerto Vallarta, Manzanillo and the oldest and much-touted Acapulco,

lure tourists to the region's seaside wonders. Here you will find the postcard version of Mexico with pristine beaches and exotic poolside cocktails at beach-hugging strings of hotels. Much of Mexico's tourism revenue is generated by the resorts along this sun-blessed stretch of Pacific coastline.

In the east is the 725km-long (450-mile) state of Veracruz. This lush, wet coastal plain has a tropical climate and is extremely fertile. The Olmecs, the earliest of Mexico's classic civilizations, settled here. Veracruz has also been Mexico's gateway to the world, a gateway Mexico may have wanted to keep closed at times. Hernán Cortés and his army of Conquistadors arrived in Veracruz in 1519. Their march to Tenochtitlán and conquest of the Aztec empire would change the face of Mexico forever.

Today Veracruz is a bustling seaport and is the epicentre of Mexico's billion-dollar oil industry. It is also the home of a huge fishing industry that supplies Mexico with a 10th of its commercial seafood.

Away from the city of Veracruz life moves at a slower pace. The great snow-capped volcano Pico de Orizaba overlooks the farms of Indians in the Los Tuxtlas mountain rainforests, fields of maize, and coffee, vanilla and tobacco plantations sweeping down to the coast where small fishing villages harvest the marine abundance of the Gulf of Mexico.

PREVIOUS PAGES:
PAGE 72: *In Jalisco, Mariachi musicians offer themselves a tequila toast.*
PAGE 73: *Cacaxtla murals from Tlaxcala. The Cacaxtla allied themselves with Spain and fought against the Aztecs.*

*On the way down from the high, arid North towards the Central Valley is Zacatecas State. The city of Zacatecas, crammed into a narrow gully between two hills at 2500m (8200ft), is a fine colonial city. Founded in 1546, it was one of Mexico's richest silver cities. For three centuries the mines of this area generated incredible wealth, and although the boom ended with the political upheavals of the 19th century, some of the best examples of Mexico's wealth of colonial architecture remain. Perhaps the most outstanding of these is the town's towering cathedral (above left and below left). Built in 1750 from the pink stone typical of the area, it is one of Mexico's best examples of late Spanish-Mexican Baroque, or Churrigueresque, architecture. Today life in this city is somewhat more sedate; a Zacatecan woman (below)* keeps her hands busy in-between selling red peppers.

A statue of Pancho Villa stands as a reminder that Zacatecas was, like much of Mexico, caught up in the 1910 revolution. In 1914 Pancho Villa defeated 12,000 government soldiers in the town. The statue, with the cry of revolution on Villa's lips, celebrates the struggle that gave Mexico its constitution.

The Zacatecas cathedral dominates the city's skyline (below). The beauty of Zacatecas (the name comes from the Náhuatl for 'place where the zacate grass grows') is enhanced by the harshness of the surrounding hills and semi-arid plains.

The Franciscan convent (opposite) is one of the oldest buildings in San Luis Potosí. San Luis was originally founded as a mission in 1592 but large silver deposits changed the city's destiny. 'Potosí' (after the rich mines of that name in Bolivia) was added to the city's name and San Luis Potosí began gathering its incredible wealth. The creation of this wealth was often at the expense of the local Indian population which was subjugated and forced to work the area's silver mines. For more than 300 years San Luis Potosí grew rich on its gold and silver mines, leaving behind a wealth of colonial architecture (below). It is the capital of the state of San Luis Potosí.

At the Museo de la Máscara (The Mask Museum) in San Luis Potosí, a fascinating collection of more than 700 masks (below) highlights the importance of the mask in Mexican culture. In Pre-hispanic times the mask was widely used for ceremonies. The mask continued to be a feature throughout the centuries of colonial rule and today is still an important part of festivals.

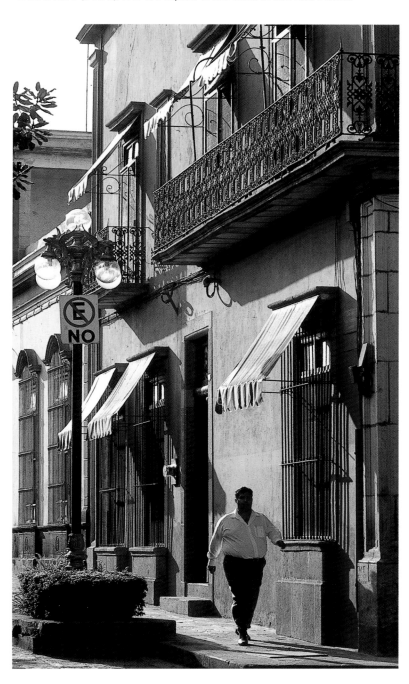

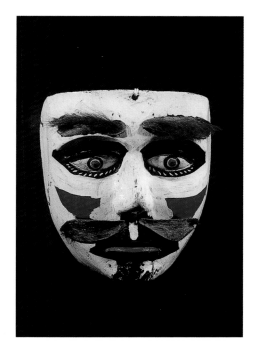

The church of Valenciana (above) in the city
of Guanajuato (below). This city, a UNESCO
World Heritage site, was founded in 1559
after large veins of silver were found in the
area. These rich veins yielded a staggering
20 per cent of the world's silver during the
15th and 16th centuries.

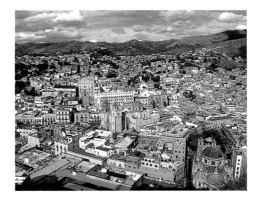

Guanajuato, capital city of Guanajuato State, boasts many grand buildings including the church of La Compañía (left), a fine example of Churrigueresque architecture. This colonial town is enlivened by the 15,000 students who attend the Guanajuato University, next door to La Compañía. In October the university hosts the annual Cervantes arts festival, when students perform one-act plays by the author of Don Quixote.

The church of San Diego (left) displays the lavish Churrigueresque style of sculpting that found a respected place in Mexican architecture. The head of Christ (top right) peers down from a shrine in the church of San Diego. The trickling blood, torn cheek, and mutilated shoulders are typical of the vivid drama seen in the statues and murals found within Mexico's churches. It is a drama quite in character with the history of the city. In 1811 Royalist forces captured the leaders of the struggle for Mexican Independence, begun by father Miguel Hidalgo in 1810 in the nearby town of Dolores Hidalgo. The men were beheaded, and their heads were displayed in metal cages on the four corners of the Alhóndiga de Granaditas building.

The house where Diego Rivera was born (right) in Guanajuato is now a museum dedicated to a Muralist of great power and idealism, and one of Mexico's best known modern artists. By the age of three, young Rivera had coloured so many of the walls in this house that his father bought him a blackboard. Rivera went on to lead the Muralist movement and covered the walls of many public buildings with his vast murals.

*San Miguel de Allende* (top left), *east of Guanajuato city, is one of a handful of Mexico's towns to have been declared a national monument. San Miguel was founded in 1542 by a Franciscan friar, acquiring the 'de Allende' in honour of one of its native sons, Ignacio de Allende, who was one of the leaders of the struggle for Mexican Independence. San Miguel de Allende prospered in colonial times, and a number of fine buildings* (above) *were constructed here by wealthy landowners. The town is also known as a cultural centre, and the arts institute, known as the Instituto Allende, has attracted many artists and writers to the town.*

*Prickly Pear Cactus leaves and fruit* (left) *for sale in San Miguel de Allende; both are eaten.*

*This church* (opposite) *in Yuriria, in southern Guanajuato State, incorporates both Pre-Columbian and Plateresque stylistic elements. The term 'Plateresque' derives from the Spanish* platero, *meaning 'silversmith', as the ornamental stonemasonry draws on the motifs of 16th-century Spanish silverware for inspiration.*

Guadalajara, capital of Jalisco State, is Mexico's second city in both size and importance. Despite its size, with a population of more than 3.5 million people, Guadalajara has retained much of its provincial charm. The city was founded in 1542, and work began on the Cathedral (opposite top) which dominates the city's zócalo in 1561. It took another century to complete the building. Next to the Cathedral is the Government Palace (opposite bottom and above) which houses the great Orozco murals. A flaming mural of Hidalgo brandishing his sword of independence (see page 39) dominates the central staircase of the palace. This mural is considered to be one of the finest examples of Orozco's work. The Hospicio Cabañas also displays some of his best murals. The Plaza Tapatía links a series of plazas that carry on throughout much of the central colonial area. The space is well used. Here mariachi bands, for which the city is famous, street performers and traders offer their wares to weekend crowds. The effect is a carnival atmosphere that makes Guadalajara one of Mexico's most pleasant cities.

A detail (right) from the elaborate kiosk in the centre of Guadalajara's zócalo area (opposite bottom). A gift from France, it is used every Thursday and Sunday when the state band occupies it to offer the people of Guadalajara lively entertainment.

*Cows graze amongst Agave cacti. The spiky plant is used to produce tequila, the quintessential Mexican drink. The leaves are removed and the juice from the pineapple-like base is distilled in a centuries-old process. The town of Tequila, about 50km (30 miles) northwest of Guadalajara, is where most of the country's tequila comes from, a head-spinning 100 million litres (176 million pints) a year.*

*A hot air balloon rises over the Pacific Ocean resort town of Puerto Vallarta (top right). In recent times this picturesque town, known for its cobbled streets and white-washed villas, has become a favourite tourist destination. An estimated 750,000 tourists visit this town each year, overwhelming the local population of 250,000.*

*An American Crocodile opens its jaws for tourists in Puerto Vallarta. In 1963 Richard Burton and Elizabeth Taylor visited the sleepy town to shoot the film* The Night of the Iguana. *It has never been the same since. Now Puerto Vallarta is one of Mexico's thriving resort towns, earning around US$300million a year.*

*A great number of tourists visit Puerto Vallarta to sample the Pacific Ocean's underwater life* (left). *Creatures such as this moray eel* (above) *thrive in the absence of industry and its attendant discharges of effluent.*

*Puerto Vallarta's harbour* (opposite top) *attracts a great many yachts. The town rests on the Bahía de Banderas (Bay of Flags), one of the largest natural bays in Mexico. Overlooked by densely forested hills, the bay boasts many miles of pristine coastline and offers excellent opportunities for waterskiing, sailing, parasailing, horse-riding and windsurfing. Further south in the state of Colima is Las Hadas* (right), *one of a series of resorts near the large port of Manzanillo. With its fantastical Moorish-style architecture, 18-hole golf course and private beach and marina, Las Hadas (The Fairies) is considered to be one of the world's top hotel resorts. This stretch of coast is renowned for game fishing, with sailfish a speciality.*

*Cempasúchil flowers (left), better known to the world as Marigolds, are spread over graves during the Day of the Dead. The flower is also traditionally used as a medication for stomach inflammation and diarrhoea.*

*The Indian towns around Lake Pátzcuaro (top) in Michoacán State still hold onto their traditions, especially when it comes to the Day of the Dead. The calaveras (above), or the grinning skeletons, are then seen everywhere.*

89

*Tarascan puppets* (left) *from Janitzio Island, which is the largest of Lake Pátzcuaro's islands. In recent times the traditional culture of its inhabitants – who like most of the Indians living around the lake subsist on fishing its waters – has made the island popular with tourists. The island is dominated by a 40m (130ft) statue of José María Morelos, a hero of Mexico's War of Independence.*

*Tarascan Indians spread graceful butterfly nets across the waters of Lake Pátzcuaro* (below). *The fishermen form a circle and dip their nets in unison to scoop up the tiny white* charales *fish.*

The Tarascan Indians are descendants of the Purépechan Indians who settled around the lake in the 14th century. The Spanish Conquistadors were very hard on these people, and in order to escape the brutality of the Spanish mines, many of the villagers learnt how to produce crafts. Different villages specialized in different products, establishing traditions that continue to this day. The Pátzcuaro area is known to produce particularly good silverware, which can be bought at markets such as this one in Pátzcuaro town (right). The town is a centre for the Tarascan Indians, and festivals and ceremonies such as this sabre dance (below) can be seen in its streets.

The pyramid (top) at Tingambato, west of Pátzcuaro, was built by Tarascan Indians as testimony to their power and influence over the region. The Tarascans were one of the few Mesoamerican groups who were not conquered by the Aztecs, a remarkable achievement considering their proximity to this warlike empire.

A ceramic statue of the Virgin of Guadelupe (above left) from the village of Ocumichi in Michoacán State. The work is typical of folk potters who produce works in clay and ceramics. For inspiration many of the folk potters turn to religious or traditional themes. Michoacán State is also known for copperware, lacquerwork and Panama hats.

*A yellow light illuminates a night vigil during the Day of the Dead celebrations in Tzintzuntzan (above), overlooking Lake Pátzcuaro. Nearby this small town of around 3000 people are the ruins of Tzintzuntzan, once an important centre in the Tarascan kingdom. The Aztecs knew the town as Huitzitzilán, or 'place of the humming bird' in the Náhuatl language.*

*This countryside (top) near the small town of Arangueo will be painted a flaming orange by the arrival of between 35 to 100 million Monarch Butterflies in winter. These butterflies (above) migrate in their millions from parts of the USA and Canada to winter in the state of Michoacán, around Arangueo, Toluca and Zitácuaro. They travel distances of more than 3200km (2000 miles) to reach the volcanic highlands of central Mexico. The Monarch Butterflies spend about half the year in Mexico, from October to April, before returning northwards for the summer.*

In the Náhuatl language 'Acapulco' means the 'place of giant reeds'. In colonial times it was a busy port, being the closest Pacific coast port to México City, but it declined in importance until its rebirth as a resort city after the Second World War. Now a wall of giant hotels lines the seashore (opposite) and the city is geared to tourism (below, top to bottom). The architect of the Hotel Princess (below, bottom) borrowed its shape from Mexico's ancient pyramids. Tourism is the foundation of Acapulco's economy, and the millions of people who visit the Pacific resort have fuelled rapid growth over the past few decades.

A tourist paraglides (right) near Acapulco, which is known for its warm clear waters and fine white beaches. This is just one of the postcard-perfect activities such as sailing, fishing, surfing and diving enjoyed by tourists at resorts along this sun-blessed coastline. One activity visitors to Acapulco will probably not take on, however, is cliff diving. A cliff diver will plunge 40m (130ft) off the high coastal cliffs of Acapulco at La Quebrada (below), timing his dive so that he lands safely in an incoming swell. In the past the divers made these death-defying leaps for ceremonial reasons. These days they dive for tourists.

Small streets snaking off from Taxco's main plaza (above) are typical scenes in this wealthy colonial silver city. However, it is not rich silver veins that make Taxco one of Mexico's wealthier towns. Taxco, in Guerrero State, is home to hundreds of highly skilled silversmiths and calls itself the silver capital of the world because of the fine silverwork produced here. There are now over 300 shops in Taxco specializing in the finely crafted silverware that attracts customers from around the world.

A panoramic view of Taxco (left) including the church of Santa Prisca, shows that the city has more to offer than just silverware. The city of 95,000 people is a romantic vision of old Spain with its cobbled stone streets and red-tiled buildings. The Churrigueresque church was commissioned by José de la Borda, a Spaniard who made his fortune after discovering silver in the area.

The small church of Santa María Tonanzintla (opposite), *tucked away in the village of Tonanzintla, around 16km (10 miles) west of Puebla city in Puebla State, is one of Mexico's best examples of Baroque architecture. Every square inch of available space of the interior of the church is covered with colourful stucco images* (above and top right). *Saints, devils, angels, flowers, fruit, birds and almost everything else dances on a gold background. Before the Spanish* arrived, the Mesoamericans created elaborate stucco works in their temples, and their methods later found expression in colonial churches. Saints peer down from the façade of the church of Santa María (above) which is relatively plain in relation to the ornate interior, although very colourful with its blue, white and red tiles.

*Mexico is a land of churches. Almost every village, town and city has some grand religious building (above), and the town of Cholula, west of Puebla city, allegedly has one for every day of the year. The church of Nuestra Señora de los Remedios (right) is built on top of the pyramid of Tenepapa, supposedly the largest structure of its kind in the world. This temple complex was a religious centre for many centuries, enduring the reigns of various Mesoamerican civilizations. It is associated with the worship of Quetzalcóatl, and was an important city until Cortés attacked it on his way to Tenochtitlán in 1519. Popocatépetl (in the background) is Mexico's second-highest peak at 5465m (17,930ft). The nearby peak of Iztaccíhuatl, at 5286m (17,343ft), is Mexico's third highest. In Aztec legend the warrior Popocatépetl ('Smoking Mountain' in Náhuatl) fell in love with Iztaccíhuatl, the emperor's daughter. When he went to war, Iztaccíhuatl died of grief. On his return Popocatépetl laid her across two mountains and stood sentinel with a burning torch. With imagination, the smoking warrior and the reclining princess can still be seen.*

A waterfall (opposite) in the beautiful and remote northern sierra of Puebla State. Hydroelectric power and mineral water are important to the economy of this state. Pueblans and visitors to the state can enjoy many natural attractions, including a volcano named La Malinche.

While it is only a few hours' drive away from the chaos of México City, the state of Puebla seems to be of another time. A large Indian population lives in the northern mountains, and their traditional embroidery-work (above) is popular with both Mexicans and visitors to the country.

*Quetzal dancers in Aztec-style costumes (above) relive the traditions of the past.
The red feathers used to make the elaborate fans are from the rare Quetzal bird
found deep within the rainforests of Oaxaca and Chiapas. In the past the Maya
trapped hundreds of Quetzal birds so they could use their beautiful red and green
feathers. It was a crime punishable by death to kill a Quetzal, and the birds were
released to grow more feathers.*

*The Colonial heartland was for centuries the stronghold of all things Spanish and the European influence is strongly felt to this day. The clash between the Mesoamerican cultures and that of the Spanish rulers resulted in a heady cocktail of traditions. Dancers (top) and tilework (above) attest to the strong Spanish influence still visible in the city of Puebla. Many of the city's colonial buildings are covered in similar hand-painted tiles for which Puebla has become famous.*

Puebla has for centuries been a staging town between México City and Veracruz and has collected a great diversity of cultures (above). Today Puebla is Mexico's fourth-largest city. Bullfighting (left) is a bequest from Mexico's Spanish past and the sport is still popular in this city, which is noted for its conservatism and allegiance to things Spanish. Puebla sided with Spain in the War of Independence, earning the city its conservative reputation.

Indian stuccowork and Puebla tiles adorn the bell tower of the church of San Francisco de Acatepec (opposite). In the 17th century tiles (azulejos) were used on church domes and building façades. These tiles came to characterize Pueblan architecture. In the 18th century an elaborate white stucco ornamentation called alfenique became popular. This lavish style, associated with a rich cake, can be seen in the Acatepec bell tower.

FOLLOWING PAGES: Views of Puebla and Veracruz states with Pico de Orizaba in the background.

An artefact from El Tajín (left) hints at the remarkable civilizations that built this city, one of the least understood of Mexico's ancient cities. El Tajín is the highest architectural achievement of the Mesoamerican civilizations in the state of Veracruz.

The main pyramid structure at El Tajín (below). The city was first occupied in 100AD but most of the main building work was carried out in 600 or 700AD. In the language of the Totonac people, the city's name means 'thunder', 'lightning' or 'hurricane', all of which are common in the tropical lowlands of Veracruz. Beyond its name little is known about the city, which was abandoned around 1200AD and only discovered by the Spanish in 1785.

*The* Voladores de Papantla *or 'flying men'* (right) *performing for the festival of Corpus Christi which coincides with an ancient harvesting festival. Four of the performers descend from the top of a 20m (65ft) pole in 13 circles. In total the four flyers revolve 52 times (13 each), a significant number in the pre-Hispanic calendar which is made up of 52 weeks. The fifth performer dances and plays music from his position at the top of the pole. The same festival of Corpus Christi is captured in the work of Diego Rivera* (below). *Rivera's work often celebrated the achievements of the Mesoamericans, such as the Totonac civilization centred on the ancient city of El Tajín shown here.*

*Until very recently Veracruz, named 'True Cross' by Hernán Cortés and his Conquistadors when they landed here in the 16th century, was Mexico's most important port (above and opposite bottom). The ports of Tampico and Coatzacoalcos, north and south of Veracruz along the Gulf coast respectively, now compete for this position. However Veracruz remains Mexico's most historic port. The great fleets carrying the astonishing mineral wealth of 'New Spain' back to Spain departed from here, and the port was subject to raids by marauding pirates including the Englishman Sir Francis Drake.*

*The colonial fort of San Juan de Ulúa (top) tells of a time when the city of Veracruz had to protect itself from the outside world. The fort is built on an island, now linked to the mainland by a road. Ever since Hernán Cortés arrived at Veracruz on Good Friday in April 1519 the city has been the gateway to Mexico. Veracruz is four times heroic: for expelling the Spanish in 1825, for the triumph over the French during the Pastry Wars and for resisting the Americans in 1847 and 1914. It is now a vibrant city with a hugely popular annual carnival during which its streets thrum to the Caribbean sounds of marimbas and steel drums.*

# THE SEAT OF POWER
## MÉXICO CITY, TEOTIHUACAN AND POPOCATÉPETL

México City is a true megalopolis. An estimated 20 million people or one-sixth of the country's population live within the greater México City area, making it the biggest urban sprawl in the world. The district is 21,355 km² (8243 sq. miles) in area, accounting for about 1.1 per cent of the national total.

Settlers first arrived in the valley around 20,000 years ago. Since then the rich volcanic soils and temperate climate have proved to be a magnet to a variety of cultures. One of the great mysteries of this area is Teotihuacán, a great city that reached its peak around 500AD. By the time the Aztecs settled in the Central Valley, it was completely deserted. Now, tourists stroll around the city's vast plaza or wonder at the great temples of the Sun and Moon. It is assumed that the city was the work of an early Toltec society, but little is known about the lives of these people as they left nothing in writing. The name 'Teotihuacán' was given to the city by the Aztecs, meaning 'Place of the Gods'.

The city of Tenochtitlán was built in answer to an Aztec prophesy at a place where Aztecs saw an eagle eating a snake on a cactus, which is today the symbol of Mexico. Built on an island in Lake Texcoco, the city was linked to the mainland by broad walkways and was lined with floating gardens. When the Spanish conquered the city in 1521AD they tore down many of the great temples and used the materials to build their own grand city. From that time onwards the city has remained the nation's capital. Today México City is the gateway to the country and the seat of power, from which the government rules over the country's 32 districts. The city has its problems, one of the biggest being high levels of pollution. Encircled by a ring of mountains, much of the considerable pollution generated by this city is trapped within the Valley of Mexico. The metropolis is also built on shaky ground, and despite the resources which first attracted people to the area, the site of modern México City was never really a good choice. Popocatépetl, the nearest volcanic peak, is active and has in recent years been smouldering and spewing out gas and cinders. Much of the city is also sinking, built as it is on reclaimed land formerly at the bottom of a lake.

México is growing at a drastic rate. Urbanization continues to attract hopefuls to the city despite the government's attempts to create other economic centres. Half a century ago, the city still retained much of its colonial charm and its population of around three million enjoyed a city of wide avenues dominated by the 688ha (1,700-acre) Chapultepec Park. Now the old historic centre is surrounded by 2600km² (1000 sq. miles) of the vibrant, hectic, intimidating and exhilarating cocktail that is Mexico's first city.

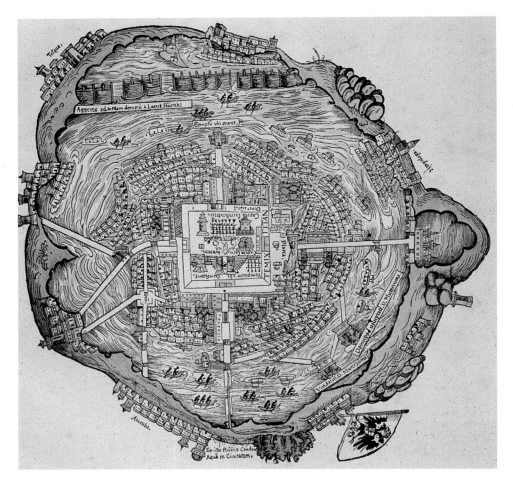

*An old map of the city of Tenochtitlán (left), one of the wonders of the Mesoamerican world. The map shows the island city with its central temple precinct and markets, surrounded by floating gardens and causeways linking the city to the shores of Lake Texcoco. It was along one of these causeways that Cortés and his men rode to meet the Aztec emperor Moctezuma II in 1519.*

PREVIOUS PAGES:
PAGE 114: *A night-time view of El Angel, which commemorates Mexico's struggle for independence, on the Paseo de la Reforma in México City.*
PAGE 115: *One of México City's fleet of cheerful green taxis.*

*The Templo Mayor (left and right), the main temple of Tenochtitlán, lay hidden beneath modern México City for centuries after having been destroyed by the Conquistadors. Many of the buildings in the Aztec city were dismantled by the Spaniards who used the rubble to build the grand capital of New Spain, which eventually became what is today México City. The Templo Mayor was rediscovered by workers in 1978, and excavations went on until 1982, leaving the scarred remains of the ancient capital of the Aztec world exposed among the colonial and modern buildings of today's capital city.*

116

*Detail of the Templo Mayor* (right) *showing Quetzalcóatl, the plumed serpent, one of the Aztec gods. When Hernán Cortés arrived in Veracruz in 1519 (coincidentally the year, in the Aztecs' cyclical conception of time, in which the pale-skinned and bearded god Quetzalcóatl was expected to return), Moctezuma thought the Spaniard might be the returning god. For this reason he didn't instruct his armies to kill the Spaniards outright, a decision which was to cost him his empire and his life.*

*Diego Rivera's mural of Tenochtitlán* (below) *is one of many commissioned by the Mexican government in the 1920s, the height of the Muralist movement which revisited Mexico's Mesoamerican past.*

The icons of the two cultures that met and clashed in Mexico are still seen throughout the country and are sharply contrasted in México City. Here Aztec dancers (opposite) and Catholic images (above) jostle for the nation's attention. The Aztec dances are more than mere shows; they are expressions of ancient traditions which have struggled to survive in modern Mexico. Images of the Virgin of Guadalupe (above and right) are seen at the Basilica of Guadalupe. A chapel was built here on the site of an Aztec temple after the dark-skinned Madonna appeared to an Indian convert in a vision. The Virgin of Guadalupe became the patron saint of Indians and Mestizos, and her image is believed to have miracle-working powers. The festival that takes place here on 12 December every year (below) is one of Mexico's most important religious festivals, and pilgrims travel great distances to visit the basilica and participate in the festivities.

The interior (left) and the exterior (below) of the cathedral on the zócalo, México City's main square. Work began on the cathedral in the 1520s, soon after the Spanish conquered the Aztec capital. The cathedral, which is Mexico's biggest, was built from material taken from the Aztecs' most sacred temple, the Templo Mayor. The El Sagrario Metropolitano (opposite bottom left), adjoining the cathedral, is built in the Churrigueresque style. This building's enormous weight is causing it to slowly sink into the spongy soil which was once the bed of Lake Texcoco, which was drained to make way for México City.

The National Palace (opposite top) is around 200m (650ft) long and occupies the entire eastern side of the zócalo, which is said to be the second-largest square in the world after Moscow's Red Square. The Aztec emperor Moctezuma II had built a palace on this site, which the Conquistadors destroyed and replaced with their own. This served as the seat of government for Cortés and subsequent viceroys. The much enlarged government complex that now occupies this site is the office of Mexico's president, close to the ceaseless activity of the zócalo (opposite bottom right).

Three vaqueros (top) *seem to have all the time in the world as they wait their turn to show off their cowboy skills in a* Charreada, *the Mexican version of a rodeo show. In México City these are often held on Sundays at the Rancho del Charro on the western side of Chapultepec Park.*

Hernán Cortés held the first bullfight in México City to celebrate the founding of New Spain. Since then bullfighting (above) has remained an important part of Mexico's Spanish heritage. The main bullring in México City (right), with its 64,000-seat arena, is the largest bullring in the world.

The Palacio de Bellas Artes (opposite) *was commissioned by Porfirio Díaz, Mexico's best remembered president. Even before it was completed, the building's heavy Carrara marble shell began sinking into the soft soil of the dried-out lake. Designed by Italian architect Adamo Boari, the building is a mixture of Art Deco, Art Nouveau and Neo-Classical styles. It has a wonderful Tiffany stained-glass stage curtain and murals by Diego Rivera, David Alfaro Siqueiros and José Clemente Orozco – known as the 'Big Three' of Mexico's Muralist movement.*

A newsstand (above), *the stock exchange* (right), *and a street vendor* (far right) *are all integral parts of the tapestry of inner city life in México City.*

*A hand-painted cloth* (left) *for sale at a Sunday market. These markets, which mushroom throughout the city on Sundays, range from a handful of stalls on the side of a road to the vast sprawling flower market held at Xochimilco. On the outskirts of the city, Xochimilco is a major vegetable and flower-growing area and still has floating gardens, or* chinampas, *which were used to grow crops in Aztec times. Boat trips on the canals in this region are a popular weekend outing for Mexican families and visitors to the city.*

*A stack of tortillas* (top), *which are thin cakes of corn or wheatmeal, and colourful fruit* (above) *add vitality to the city streets. Food stalls are found throughout the city, and tortillas — which can be made quickly and filled with a wide variety of fillings — are particularly popular. There is a great variety of fresh fruit and fruit drinks to choose from, including pineapples, oranges, limes, watermelons, papayas and guavas.*

*An artefact* (above) *from a little understood past. Even the Aztecs who ruled over Central Mexico in the 14th and 15th centuries did not know the origins of the people who built Teotihuacán. The Aztecs made pilgrimages to this city, which they believed to have been inhabited by gods.*

*A detail from the ruins of Teotihuacán* (opposite bottom left). *This ancient city, famous for its temples of the Sun and the Moon, lies 50km (30 miles) north of México City. Little is known about the civilization of the people who inhabited the city. During the 2nd century BC, a collection of villages formed in this area, and work began on the great city at around the time of Christ. By 600AD Teotihuacán had a population of about 200,000 people inhabiting an area of around 22km$^2$ (8.5 sq. miles), making it the sixth-largest city in the world at the time. The Temple of the Sun* (top centre) *is the third-largest pyramid in the world. It took some three million tons of stone to build the 70m-high (230ft) pyramid. This was done without the use of pack animals, metal tools or the wheel. The great Avenue of the Dead* (left) *runs in a north-south direction for about 4km (2.5 miles). This strip of temples was given the name Teotihuacán, meaning 'Place of the Gods', by the Aztecs, who believed that the buildings lining the avenue were vast tombs built by giants for Teotihuacán's first rulers. The Aztecs believed that the city was abandoned after Teotihuacán's gods had sacrificed themselves to create the sun and the moon. In October 1998 archaeologists discovered a burial chamber inside the Temple of the Moon. The human skeleton and artifacts they found may begin to help us unravel the secrets of this mysterious city.*

*Popocatépetl Volcano took its present shape* (above) *about 2.5 million years ago during the great convulsions that shook central Mexico. After more than half a century of silence the volcano came to life again in 1993, and since then 'El Popo', as it is known, occasionally belches gas and plumes of ash. It is closed for climbing and the villages that surround its slopes have evacuation plans ready in case it begins to spew mud and cinders over them. A major eruption would endanger hundreds of thousands of people living in these villages and the nearby city of Puebla (less than 30km, or 18 miles, away), and the volcano is carefully monitored by the National Disaster Prevention Centre (CENAPRED).*

# THE LUSH SOUTH

## OAXACA, CHIAPAS AND TABASCO

Oaxaca is where North American Mexico and Central American Mexico break with each other. Here the two arms of the Sierras converge into a single range that pushes on through Central America and then rises as the great Andes mountain range. The sometimes barren landscapes of northern Mexico are replaced with thickly forested rolling hills and low-lying swamps and jungles. This area is one of the wettest in Mexico. Fifteen per cent of Mexico's rainfall gathers in the basins of Chiapas State alone. Together Oaxaca and Chiapas cover 168,163km² (65,000 sq. miles), just under nine per cent of the national total.

Much of this area is crossed by mountain ranges. In Oaxaca the Sierra Madre del Sur, the Sierra Madre de Oaxaca and the Sierra Atravesada dominate the land. The average heights along these ranges are between 2000 and 2500m (6560 and 8200ft). The Sierra Madre de Chiapas dominates Chiapas, running southeast to its highest point, the Tacaná Volcano (4060m; 13,320ft) on the border of Guatemala.

Within these states are some of Mexico's least developed areas. However, while development may be sluggish, indigenous cultures thrive. Traditional lifestyles carry on here as if the conquest and all that was to follow had never occurred. Deep in the jungles the Mixtec, Zapotec and Lacandón Indians continue to live traditionally. They live without electricity and not a word of Spanish is spoken in many villages. Oaxaca and Chiapas have Mexico's biggest proportion of Indians in their populations. In the latter state alone there are about 750,000 Indians out of a total of around 3.5 million people.

The state of Chiapas captured world headlines with the Zapatista uprising on New Year's day in 1994. Several thousand armed rebels wearing black balaclavas occupied San Cristóbal and declared war on the Mexican government. The movement demanded land reform and the resignation of the Mexican president of the day. Although the occupation lasted only 30 hours, it touched a nerve in the Mexican nation, one that has always been sensitive to land issues.

This area is rich in wildlife and home to one of the last stretches of North American rainforest. The Montes Azules Biosphere Reserve, which surrounds the Mayan ruins at Bonampak, provides refuge for exotic creatures such as jaguars, spider monkeys, and tapirs. Also fighting the forces of change are the Lacandón Indians. They retreated into these forests to avoid persecution by the Spanish and have remained there ever since. They refer to themselves as *Hach Winik*, or True People. The 'Lacandón' label was coined by the Spanish to describe any group of Indians living outside of colonial control.

PREVIOUS PAGES:

PAGE 130: *A Lacandón Indian, one of the last few hundred who live in the Chiapas rainforests.*

PAGE 131: *A Zapotec Indian, a member of the largest group of Indians in the state of Oaxaca.*

*The town of Oaxaca* (opposite bottom) *has had a relatively quiet history since the Spanish conquest. Porfirio Díaz, later president of the Republic, was born here in 1830. The church of Santo Domingo* (opposite top), *built in the 1570s, was considered by Aldous Huxley to be 'one of the most extravagantly gorgeous churches in the world'. Few areas of the interior of this building have escaped the exuberant decorations that make this one of Oaxaca's most prized places of worship.*

*Monte Albán* (above) *stands upon a mountain (the name means 'white mountain') overlooking Oaxaca's three valleys, and is one of Mexico's most impressive archaeological sites The building of this ambitious city, which at its peak had a population of around 35,000, began around the 7th century BC. During the many centuries that Monte Albán was inhabited, a number of groups lived in the great city, but it was probably most developed by the Zapotecs and later the Mixtecs. The origin and meaning of the famous Danzantes* (right), *carved stone slabs used to decorate the Building of Dancers, are much debated.*

The state of Oaxaca is home to one-fifth of Mexico's indigenous Indian population. The influence of the Indian cultures and aesthetics can be felt throughout this region, especially during the many festivals. These three dancing figures, carved from radishes, celebrate a harvest festival.

Colourful bags brighten the village market in Tlacolula (opposite top). A number of villages around the city of Oaxaca host a market on separate days of the week, each specializing in different products. The Sunday market in Tlacolula, the busiest in the region, specializes in ceramics and hand-woven rugs. Tlacolula is located in one of three valleys that radiate out from the city of Oaxaca. The valley that runs in an easterly direction has a mostly Zapotec population, such as this local man and woman (opposite bottom left and right).

A street scene in Ocotlán (above) is typical of the rural atmosphere pervading this region. All of this changes during market day when the village is transformed into a bustling centre. Ocotlán specializes in reed mats. These terracotta figurines of young women bearing colourful fruit (right) are echoes of the ancient Mesoamerican fertility themes. The vibrant pieces were also made in Ocotlán.

*A farmer herding his livestock near Asunción. Many of the people living in the valleys of Oaxaca grow cash crops and keep livestock. They sell ceramics, leatherwork, food and flowers at village markets. It is a lifestyle that has changed very little over the centuries.*

*Oaxaca Valley (top) is the most populated and cultivated in the southern highlands. The spiky Agave Cactus (above) is one of the Maguey Cacti and is commonly used to make tequila. The plant is also used to make Oaxaca's favourite drink, mescal – famously known for the worm in the bottle. Pulque, a less alcoholic drink made from these cacti, predates the arrival of the Spanish. It has a lower alcohol content than tequila or mescal.*

Cooking at home (above). An Aztec Codex (right) shows the ancient cooking methods used centuries ago, which are not very different to those used in Oaxaca today – for instance the Oaxacan woman kneading dough into tortillas (opposite).

Chocolate (below) is also one of Mexico's time-worn culinary traditions. Made from the cacao pod, chocolate was known to have been drunk by Aztec emperor Moctezuma II, who introduced it to the Spaniards.

The once sleepy village of Huatulco (above) *is destined to join the ranks of Mexico's other big resort towns. In recent years the Mexican government has aimed its resources at developing the fishing town into a major resort. When completed, it will be the government's biggest tourist project since Cancún. A number of international hotels have already appeared as well as the luxury homes of a few of the rich and famous, including the singer Julio Iglesias. Visitors to the resort can still enjoy uncrowded beaches along its nine jungle-fringed bays, and there are excellent opportunities for diving and other water sports. Surfing the Pacific waves (left) is particularly popular.*

The fishing village of Puerto Escondido (Hidden Port) is nestled within a sheltered bay (above) and is surrounded by hills covered with lush vegetation. Around 260km (160 miles) due south of Oaxaca town, this is one of Mexico's resort towns that has yet to grow up into a major tourist centre, and it still has that get-away-from-it-all feeling. The area is particularly known for its good surfing conditions. Puerto Ángel (right) is an old fishing village and former coffee port tucked away in one of Oaxaca's southern coast bays, around 80km (50 miles) southeast of Puerto Escondido. The village is a favourite amongst backpackers who are drawn to its pristine beaches and laid-back atmosphere.

*The last major remaining tracts of Mexican rainforest are found in the Lacandón Jungle (left). The rainforest that stretches between San Cristóbal and Palenque covers an area of about 10,000km$^2$ (3860 sq. miles).*

*The waterfalls in the state of Chiapas (below) are said to be the most spectacular in the whole of Mexico. The combination of natural beauty and diversity of wildlife draws many visitors to this southern state.*

Chiapas provides a sanctuary for a large percentage of Mexico's bio-diversity. Ecotourism is a growth industry here, with people coming to visit areas like the Montes Azules Biosphere Reserve in the southeast. They are treated to a range of rare and unusual plants and creatures, from orchids to tapirs, toucans to howler monkeys. Pharmaceutical companies are funding research here into substances which they can synthesize and market as useful drugs.

In the highlands north of San Cristóbal lies the village of San Juan Chamula. The parish church here is a centre of worship for the Chamulan Indians. Its décor and ceremonies, such as this purification ceremony (left), are striking examples of the mixture of Catholic-Christian and Mayan beliefs which characterize religion in the region. The carnival in Tenejapa (below), and a festival at Zinacantán (bottom), are also good examples of traditional Indian religious gatherings in villages close to San Cristóbal. The many groups of Indians living in this region can be distinguished by the colours and styling of the clothes they wear, as well as the ribbons on their differently styled straw hats.

FOLLOWING PAGES: *Indians relaxing in the village of San Juan Chamula.*

Detail of a wall carving (left) from Palenque, one of Mexico's most magical ancient cities. The Mayan city was first occupied over 1500 years ago and reached its greatest period between the 7th and 9th centuries. Sometime in the 9th century Palenque was abandoned. The surrounding Lacandón jungles soon hid the ancient city and it was forgotten until the 18th century. In 1949 a secret passageway was found in the Temple of the Inscriptions (below left). Years of hard excavation work revealed a series of tunnels and chambers, leading archaeologists to the sensational discovery in 1952 of the tomb of the Mayan ruler Pacal. The Temple of the Inscriptions at Palenque is one of 38 structures that have been excavated so far. The rest (the estimated total number of buildings in the complex is 500) have yet to be reclaimed from the surrounding jungles. There is no telling what archaeologists may still find. As impressive as the Temple of the Sun (below) still is, it must have appeared even grander in its heyday – when the temples were painted vermilion and the city was the heart of a vast empire.

As is the case at many other Mayan sites, the temples of Palenque also served as giant timepieces. Archaeologists speculate that the tower that crowns the Palace buildings (above) at Palenque was used to observe the sun falling directly into the Temple of Inscriptions during the winter solstice (22 December).

A detail from a Mayan mural (right) shows what may have been a sacrificial ritual. There is evidence that the Maya practised human sacrifice, but not nearly on the same scale as the Aztecs. Probably the finest Mayan murals are found at the remote ruins at Bonampak in eastern Chiapas, near the border with Guatemala.

*Tourists enjoy a boat ride on a river in Tabasco* (opposite top). *The rivers of this humid state feed a number of lakes, swamps and lush tropical jungles.*

*A colonial house undergoes repairs in Villahermosa* (opposite bottom), *capital city of Tabasco State. The city has undergone similar renovations, largely funded by revenues from the state's abundant oil reserves. Now the boom-town is known for tree-shaded boulevards, parks and cultural institutions. A boy pauses in wonder before a giant Olmec head* (above right) *in the excellent open-air museum in Villahermosa.*

*A portrait of a man from rural Tabasco* (top left), *and harvesting cacao pods* (bottom left). *The economy of this region has switched from being an agricultural one — with the farming of crops like cacao, bananas and sugar cane — to industry after the discovery of oil. However, oil has also funded improved technology for agriculture.*

# THE YUCATAN PENINSULA
## CAMPECHE, YUCATAN AND QUINTANA ROO
## INCLUDING CANCUN

The three states that make up the Yucatán – Campeche, Yucatán and Quintana Roo – are distinctly different to the rest of Mexico. Physically the 9,426km² (53,818 sq. mile) area is dominated by a vast peninsula. This hot, flat plain rises only a few hundred metres above sea level. There are few rivers in this area and surface water is scarce. Much of the region's water is underground, stored in natural water reservoirs within the limestone rock. These underground water sources were known as *cenotes* by the early Mayan people and were crucial to their survival. The area is still the home of Mexico's 900,000 indigenous Maya.

The peninsula, made remote by poor transport routes, was isolated from the rest of the country until the 1960s when rail and road connections formed links with the rest of Mexico. Despite better transport routes, however, the Yucatán continues to exist within itself. The Maya were the last to be conquered by the Spanish and to this day have a sense of independence, separating them from the rest of Mexico. The Mayan language is still spoken in these parts and Mayan traditions have remained intact.

The Maya have inhabited this area and neighbouring Belize and Guatemala for thousands of years. Despite a harsh landscape with little water, thin soils and excessive heat, they left behind great cities, many of which have yet to be fully excavated. In the Yucatán, the greatest of these ruins are at Chichén Itzá and Uxmal. Here the greatest achievements of the Mayan civilization can be seen. The Maya developed an advanced calendar that combined solar, astronomical and religious dates into a complex and accurate system. They also developed a sophisticated mathematical system and made use of a hieroglyphics writing system that is still being deciphered today.

In more recent times tourism has made inroads into the Yucatán. The mega-resort at Cancún – ideally situated on an island in the warm, clear waters of the Caribbean with excellent opportunities for diving and water sports such as windsurfing – has become the playground of package tourists, attracting much-needed revenue to the area. The hotel-studded strip generates a quarter of Mexico's tourism revenue. Since the 1970s, when the resort was built, more than 150,000 Yucatecans have made the journey to Cancún in search of work.

Away from the hustle and bustle is the city of Mérida. Its grand colonial buildings are a reminder of boom years when the Henequén Cactus grown in the area supplied much of the fibre needed for the world's twine and rope. Synthetic materials replaced this, but Mérida continues to be the peninsula's largest city.

*Palm trees* (opposite top) *characterize the coast at the city of Campeche, on the Gulf of Mexico on the western rim of the Yucatán Peninsula. The capital of Campeche State is an interesting mixture of colonial elegance and bustling port. The thick walls of the Campeche Fort* (above) *were built to defend the city against raids by pirates, and underground passages where women and children hid from the marauders can still be seen today. Additional walls, 2.5 km (1.5 miles) long and reaching up to 8m (26ft) high, were built after a concerted attack by an armada of pirates in 1663. Today Campeche enjoys more peaceful times and welcomes visitors to sample its laid back Yucatecan way of life.*

*Next to oil, fishing* (opposite bottom and right) *is one of Campeche's few industries. The waters off this state are rich in marine life, from fishes like mackerel and tuna to an abundance of shellfish and crustacea.*

PREVIOUS PAGES:
PAGE 154: *The Pyramid of Kukulkán at Chichén Itzá.*
PAGE 155: *Fishing boat at Champotón, Campeche State.*

The southeast of Campeche State receives heavy rainfall, and has the thickest jungles on the Yucatán Peninsula. The Calakmul Biosphere Reserve has been established here to protect what is left of the Petén rainforests, which extend south into Guatemala and east into Belize. These forests are still prowled by sleek-footed jaguars (above), once considered to be gods by the Maya, hunting for deer, tapir, monkeys, coatimundis and other exotic game. The great trees and many flowering and fruiting plants also provide the ideal habitat for a host of birds including hummingbirds, trogons, honeycreepers and these Scarlet Macaws (right).

The city of Edzná flourished in the Classic Period of the Maya, from around the 5th to the early 9th century. The impressive but rather austere building style is well illustrated by the Temple of Five Levels (opposite). During the early Post-Classic period, between the 9th and 12th centuries, the Mayan civilization collapsed. Many of the great Mayan cities were invaded by Northern Toltecs and the Maya retreated into the jungles.

*The Quadrangle of the Nuns in Uxmal* (above), *which consists of 74 rooms, may have been a military academy. This ruined Mayan city, around 80km (50 miles) south of Mérida, in Yucatán State, prospered in the 9th and 10th centuries. Although the glyphs* (below) *found here are now being deciphered by archaeologists, very few written records of this time remain as the Spanish burnt them.*

*The Quadrangle of the Nuns* (below). *The first account of Uxmal came from a Spanish priest, Father Alonso Ponce, during the 16th century. Like many that followed, it was largely inaccurate.*

*The Pyramid of the Magician* (right), *so-called because of a room at the top of the 39m-high (128ft) structure that was thought to be used by priests. The Maya had to be able to predict the seasons because they had to rely on rainfall as a result of the lack of groundwater in the region. To accomplish this they built structures that enabled them to monitor time and keep track of the seasons by recording the solstices. The Mayan priests could then tell the people when to plant their crops.*

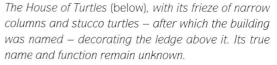

*A detail of the House of Turtles* (below) *shows examples of the stucco reliefs occurring throughout Uxmal. The most common figure is Chac, the god believed to bring the rain. In return the Maya honoured Chac and even offered the rain god human sacrifices.*

*The House of Turtles* (below), *with its frieze of narrow columns and stucco turtles – after which the building was named – decorating the ledge above it. Its true name and function remain unknown.*

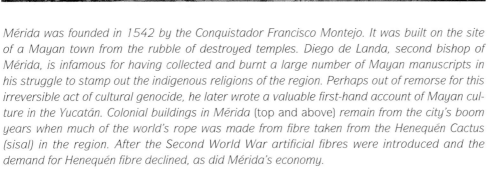

*Mérida was founded in 1542 by the Conquistador Francisco Montejo. It was built on the site of a Mayan town from the rubble of destroyed temples. Diego de Landa, second bishop of Mérida, is infamous for having collected and burnt a large number of Mayan manuscripts in his struggle to stamp out the indigenous religions of the region. Perhaps out of remorse for this irreversible act of cultural genocide, he later wrote a valuable first-hand account of Mayan culture in the Yucatán. Colonial buildings in Mérida* (top and above) *remain from the city's boom years when much of the world's rope was made from fibre taken from the Henequén Cactus (sisal) in the region. After the Second World War artificial fibres were introduced and the demand for Henequén fibre declined, as did Mérida's economy.*

Festivals in Mérida (above) are almost weekly affairs. Mérida is the capital of the state of Yucatán and the largest of the Yucatán Peninsula's cities. Yucatecan festivals draw on the traditions of the 900,000 indigenous Maya living in the region, and are displays of the Maya's cultural independence. The Spanish Conquistadors had to fight very hard to subdue the Maya in the Peninsula, and it took them decades to establish control over only around half of it. Mexican Independence in 1821 sparked off a wave of secessionist movements in the Yucatán, and a series of rebellions, ending only in the 20th century. The region remained effectively cut off from the rest of Mexico until rail links and better roads were established in the 1950s.

The Pyramid of Kukulkán (above) at Chichén Itzá, one of Mexico's best preserved Mesoamerican sites. Kukulkán is Mayan for 'Plumed Serpent', the Toltec god who displaced the Mayan rain god as chief deity. The pyramid is a giant calendar which has 365 steps, the same number as the days of the solar calendar used by the Maya. On the equinoxes (March 21 and September 21/22), the shadows cast by the sun as it sinks resemble a giant snake slithering down the side of the temple. A helmeted soldier chiselled into the walls of the Jaguar Temple (left) may tell of the war between the Maya and the Toltecs. In the 10th century Chichén Itzá was invaded by the Toltecs, who brought with them their god, Quetzalcóatl. The city prospered under the Toltecs, who left their stamp on its architecture — for instance the many warlike friezes, and sculptures of Quetzalcóatl (see above, at left).

The Observatory and the Pyramid of Kukulkán at Chichén Itzá (above) *rise above the dry plains of central Yucatán State. The Observatory is also known as the* Caracol, *or 'snail', for its round shape and internal spiral ramp to the top. It is believed that priests used this structure to predict the coming of the rains. A nearby* cenote, *a natural reservoir of water trapped in subterranean limestone tunnels and caves, provided the only available water. In times of drought human sacrifices and precious objects would be taken along a processional way to this* cenote *and thrown in. Toltec offerings to the gods were placed on a reclining stone figure (right),* known as a Chacmool.